Letters from North America

1. Xántus in the Uniform of the United States Navy, lithograph, 1861.

Title of original edition: Levelei Észak Amerikábol
(Budapest, 1857).
Copyright © 1975 by Wayne State University Press,
Detroit, Michigan 48202. All rights are reserved.
No part of this book may be reproduced without
formal permission.

Library of Congress Cataloging in Publication Data

Xántus, János, 1825–1894.
   Letters from North America.

   Translation of Levelei Éjszakamerikából.
   Bibliography: p.
   1. United States—Description and travel—1848–1865.
2. Xántus, János, 1825–1894.   I. Title.
E166.X3413   917.3′04′6   75–25679
ISBN 0–8143–1548–8

Letters from North America

by

John Xántus

translated and edited by
Theodore Schoenman
and Helen Benedek Schoenman
with an Introduction by Theodore Schoenman

Wayne State University Press   Detroit, 1975

to Ralph

Contents

Illustrations

Prefatory Note

Alexis de Tocqueville's classic study, *Democracy in America* (*De la Démocratie en Amérique*) provided the Western world with a penetrating and memorable insight into the nature and operation of American institutions. For a more restricted but perhaps more interested audience—that of the Austro-Hungarian Empire, and Hungary in particular—three pioneer travelers and observers of the American scene in the period before the Civil War have performed a similar service.

Alexander Farkas de Bölön and Ágoston Haraszthy, founder of the California wine industry, each wrote a book, and John Xántus, the naturalist, wrote two. All these works are eloquent evidence of their respective talents for keen observation and graphic descriptive powers.

Unlike de Tocqueville, whose work was highly critical, these Hungarians wrote with undisguised admiration for America. Although many features of American life strongly appealed to him, de Tocqueville believed in the intellectual supremacy of the elite whereas the Hungarians expressed sympathy for and approval of the unpolished but energizing élan of America's common clay. The consequent contrast in social views is both engaging and significant.

The books were all published in Hungary but, inexplicably, 10 never in English. They include *Journey in North America* (1834) by

Farkas, *Travels in North America* (1844) by Haraszthy, and the two exceptional works by Xántus, *Travels in Southern California* (1860) and the volume before us, *Letters from North America*, first published in Hungarian in 1857, which begins this series we now present to the English-reading public a century later.

We feel confident that American folk and natural history will be enhanced by these fresh and unspoiled accounts of a nation in formation and that students of Indian and settler history alike will be enlightened.

Our special thanks are due to Elain P. Halperin, editor, Wayne State University Press, for spending long and devoted hours to whip the manuscript into shape and prepare it for publication.

Xántus's illustrations are reproduced by courtesy of the Library Audiovisual and Photographic Services, University of California, Los Angeles, California.

Helen Benedek Schoenman
Theodore Schoenman

Santa Barbara
October 1973.

Introduction

The 1967 summer issue of the *New Hungarian Quarterly*, an English-language literary review published in Budapest, printed an article by László Országh entitled "California Revisited." The author, a literary historian and philologist, had done research in the Huntington Library in Pasadena and was reporting on the heady experience of revisiting America thirty-five years later. Országh's article begins:

> The first Hungarian ever to set foot in California and leave a still readable account was János Xántus, a veteran of the 1849 Hungarian War of Independence. In the early eighteen fifties Xántus made his way to America where he entered the service of the Geodetic Survey of the United States. Two books, both in Hungarian, published in Budapest over a hundred years ago, testify to his keen eye for observation and graphic descriptive power: *Letters from North America* (1857) and *Travels in Southern California* (1860). In them one may catch a somewhat startling glimpse of the infancy of California.

Like Aurel Stein and Ármin Vámbéry, who traveled the Orient, Vámbéry disguised as a dervish in Bokhara and Samarkand, Xántus is in the romantic tradition of Hungarian naturalists and explorers. Alex Farkas de Bölön as well as Ágoston Haraszthy had visited North America in the 1840s; Haraszthy subsequently established the wine industry in California. But these two men are a far cry from Xántus. Their dry and sober records cannot be compared to Xántus's flamboyant and far-ranging accounts, and they did nothing to match his achievements in the natural sciences.

It is odd that Xántus's contributions to natural history, ornithology, and the zoological sciences, which were based on explorations in North America, should have failed until now to prompt an English translation of his writings. It is true that the two Hungarian books which contain the only published accounts of his American adventures are extremely rare, being available solely in a few collections: Princeton's Firestone Library; the Bancroft Library at the University of California, Berkeley; Yale; the University of California, Los Angeles; and the New York and Los Angeles public libraries. The fact that these works are in the Hungarian language may further account for the neglect of this important contributor of huge collections of naturalia to the United States National Museum and the Smithsonian Institution.[1]

E. E. Hume begins his biography of John Xántus by noting: "Details of the romantic career of this gifted naturalist have been gathered with the greatest difficulty."[2] And H. M. Madden, in his monograph on Xántus, writes: "Of his early childhood nothing is known . . . The career of Xántus in America from 1851 to 1857 is almost as obscure as his childhood."[3]

A shroud of mystery and vagueness, which Xántus seems to have deliberately fostered, surrounds his early years in America. Yet he was highly ambitious and thirsted for recognition. During the years of his anonymous struggle to survive, he displayed in his letters to his family a pathetic tendency toward self-aggrandizement.

János (called John in America) Xántus was born on October 5, 1825, at Csokonya, in the county of Somogy. His father, Ignac, was a solicitor, land agent, and steward on the estate of Count Széchényi. János received his early education at the Benedictine gymnasium in Györ, graduating in 1841. He then studied at the Academy of Law in Györ and served three years as a vice-notary (an important position at that time) in the county of Somogy.

In 1847, he took his bar examinations in Pest and passed them. Then he returned to Csokonya and might have become a country lawyer had not the cataclysm of the Hungarian Revolution forced him to leave his country.

Let us go back at this point and see what was happening in   13

Hungary. The impact of the French Revolution and the Napoleonic era had measurably lessened the isolation of Hungary. They gave rise to a fervent Magyar cultural revival and helped to stiffen national resistance to the absolutism of the imperial court in Vienna. The policy of the Hapsburg rulers was to maintain the feudal state, and in this they had the full cooperation of the landowning aristocracy in Hungary. They succeeded even though the concurrent effort to foist a centralized German bureaucracy on the country was frustrated by the large class of small gentry which controlled local government through its traditional administration of the counties. The Vienna court saw in Hungary a country that shouldered less than its share of common burden by resisting demands for a large standing army, cash, and foodstuffs. Prince Metternich, the chief architect of the Holy Alliance, considered Hungary's insistence on its historic constitution a threat to monarchical principles. In Metternich's political philosophy, monarchy had to be absolute. Constitutional monarchy was therefore a contradiction in terms and a mask for popular sovereignty which was the offspring of revolution and the matrix of anarchy.

The Diet of 1825, which most Hungarian historians call the first Diet of the "Reform Era," reflected the burgeoning national spirit in its refusal to meet the court's demands for recruits and money. Nothing was said, however, about social reforms and the problem of the peasantry. On these issues the Diet was fully as reactionary as the crown. The principal idea was resistance to the court's absolutism.

When the Diet again assembled in 1832, its mood had undergone a radical change. This was due to two factors. One was the aftermath of a devastating cholera epidemic which had led to bloody peasant uprisings against the feudal magnates. The deputies had begun to realize the explosive urgency of dealing with the peasant issue. The other factor was the rise of Count István Széchényi, one of the most important figures in the period of Hungary's emergence from its backward feudal state. A member of a great aristocratic family, he had traveled widely in western Europe and England. In 1830 he published his famous book, *Hitel (Credit)*, in which he argued convincingly that not foreign domination but the sacrosanct constitution of the nobility was the ultimate cause of the country's backwardness. It was the sloth, selfishness, and complacency of the aristocracy that hindered the nation's progress. Széchényi suggested no far-reaching political re-

14   medies, certainly nothing like the introduction of Western democracy,

which he thought dangerous for Hungary. His program was essentially a series of economic reforms from above. Because he advocated the removal of the nobility's historic tax exemption, he was bitterly denounced as a traitor to his class. In vain did he plead with Metternich for support. Metternich snubbed young Széchényi's inpassioned pleas for reforms initiated from above in collaboration with Vienna. " 'No, no!' Metternich replied, 'take one stone out of the vaulting and the whole thing collapses,' thus dampening in advance all Széchényi's hopes."[4] The court backed the stubborn resistance of the magnates, now united by their fear of any change in the status quo.

But Széchényi's critique of the constitution found widespread support in the Diet, especially among members of the small, mostly landless gentry. The backwash of the July 1830 revolution in France and the smuggled writings of the French liberals of the day—Victor Hugo, Thiers, LaMennais, and others—exercised widespread influence. By 1835 a considerably more radical program had developed which included, besides Széchényi's demands, popular representation and parliamentary control of the budget. Széchényi's reforms by this time appeared too gradual and mild, and before the Diet adjourned the young radicals had found a dynamic leader and spokesman in the person of Lajos Kossuth, who was soon to drive Széchényi out of the field.

Kossuth, scion of an old impoverished family belonging to the gentry, was a magnificent orator, one of the most persuasive spellbinders of history. His emotional appeal was irresistible to all audiences and he was no less gifted with his pen, having an extraordinary talent for enlisting his readers' sympathy for whatever cause he was pleading.

Kossuth's first priority was national liberation. Full social and political liberty must be postponed pending elimination of the illegitimate rule of Vienna. His program quickly achieved immense popularity.

The threatening development of such an ultraliberal movement forced Metternich's hand. Kossuth was arrested for a press offense and sentenced to four years of imprisonment. The same punishment was meted out to Baron Wesselényi, another popular hero. Two years later, however, in 1839, the court had to back down and make concessions in order to obtain new recruits and supplies of grain. Kossuth and Wesselényi were amnestied; limited press freedom was granted.

The pressures and tensions in all parts of the empire finally reached a crescendo in the opening weeks of 1848. The fuse was ignited in Paris, and it touched off revolutions in Italy, Germany, and Austria. Kossuth, in a fiery speech, called for the transformation of the absolutist system into a constitutional regime not only for Hungary but for every part of the empire. Kossuth's address triggered a massive uprising in Vienna led by students. The local garrison panicked. By firing on the demonstrating masses, it further infuriated them. The court, unable to control the rioters, gave in and accepted their demands, chief among which was the dismissal of Metternich, who fled to England.

The news of Metternich's fall electrified Budapest. A group of young students known as "The Youth of Pest," led by the poet Petöfy and the novelist Jókai, organized a mass demonstration which adopted by acclamation a petition to the National Assembly. Consisting of twelve points, it embodied Kossuth's program. The Diet quickly approved and a provisional cabinet was formed that included both Kossuth and Széchényi. When the resolution of the National Assembly was presented in Vienna, the court, fearing an open revolution, conceded practically on all points and on April 11, Emperor Ferdinand I formally sanctioned the so-called April Laws. But the situation soon changed. Radetzky's victories in Lombardy encouraged the court camarilla to seek a show-down with the rebellious Magyars. The April Laws were abrogated and at the same time the Ban (viceroy) of Croatia, who had a powerful army, was incited to attack the southern district of Hungary. The imperial army under Prince Windischgrätz, ready to march, massed in the west.

Kossuth acted with dispatch. The assembly invested him with quasi-dictatorial powers. A small force of the home guard routed the Croats. This provided Kossuth with the needed breathing space to raise a large army. At this point, another bloody uprising in Vienna forced the abdication of the ineffectual Emperor Ferdinand I, and Francis Joseph, his eighteen-year-old nephew, ascended the throne which he was to occupy for sixty-eight years. The change of dynasty without consultation with the Diet represented a violation of the Magyar constitution. This, together with the new emperor's tough message to the Austrian parliament confirming absolute rule, was practically a declaration of war on Hungary. Windischgrätz, with a large army, was now on the march and for a while met scant resistance, but soon the military tide turned. After several inconclusive engagements, the Hungarians under the skillful guidance of a former imperial officer, Arthur Görgey, inflicted painful defeats and pushed Windischgrätz back beyond Hungary's borders. On April 14, 1849, the National Assembly declared Hungary an independent state, deposing the House of Hapsburg from the Magyar throne and appointing Kossuth president-regent.

The successes of the Magyar armies convinced the Austrian generals that they could not win without outside help. Francis Joseph thereupon appealed to Tsar Nicholas I for assistance. Nicholas, apprehensive of the possible effect of the Hungarian movement for national independence on Poland, complied. A large Russian force crossed into Transylvania and attacked the Hungarians from the rear. By August 1849, the fate of the out-numbered and out-gunned Hungarians was sealed. Görgey surrendered to the Russians. Kossuth fled to Turkey and later to England; this was followed by a triumphant tour of America where he received a welcome as warm as the one that had been accorded to Lafayette.

At home the most brutal and bloody reprisals followed the surrender. Defying horrified protests from the West, Francis Joseph approved the punitive measures of General Haynau, the Austrian military commander who was notorious for his pathological brutality. Thirteen general officers were hanged at Arad. Two hundred and thirty-one other high-ranking officers, together with the prime minister, Count Batthányi, were executed by firing squads. Görgey was spared only because of the tsar's intervention. Thousands were imprisioned. Many junior officers, who had been civilians before the outbreak of hostilities, were conscripted into the imperial army as privates and sent to serve outside of Hungary. Among these was János Xántus.

Xántus joined the revolutionary army and fought in the artillery as a sergeant. Later he served in the infantry and rose to the rank of first lieutenant.

Captured by the Austrians in February 1849, he was imprisoned at Königgrätz. When the war ended, the Austrians stripped him of his military rank and pressed him into the service of the Hapsburgs as a private. But his mother's money and influence secured his release. Instead of returning at once to his home town in July 1850, Xántus joined a group of Hungarian emigrés at Dresden in Saxony. There 17 unfortunately his fervent patriotic declarations were overheard. On his way home he was arrested in Prague and condemned to serve in the regiment from which he had been recently released. Xántus escaped on foot to Teschen and from there to Saxony. He continued on to Hamburg and London, and on May 5, 1851, sailed for America.[5]

In the wake of the social and political upheaval in western and central Europe in 1848-49—the February revolution in France, the liberal and national risings throughout the Italian peninsula, the revolutions in Germany for political freedom and national unification, and the revolutionary struggles for independence within the Hapsburg Empire—a large number of political refugees had sought sanctuary in the New World. Unquestionably, John Xántus was one of the most remarkable of these.

He came ashore in New York with seven dollars in his pocket. Although he spent only thirteen years in this country—from 1851 to 1864—he made a name for himself and rendered a lasting service to the natural history of America. From 1855 to 1864, as a naturalist and explorer on the western frontier, which until then had been *terra incognita*, he added immeasurably to our zoological and general knowledge of the region.

The first years of Xántus's activites in America are veiled: very few facts are ascertainable. He wrote letters to his mother describing in great detail his progress from one responsible position to another, whereas in actual fact he was frequently reduced to working at the most menial jobs. He probably spent several years in St. Louis and New Orleans. Employed as an engineering draftsman on the Pacific Railroad of Missouri survey to California, he received two dollars a day for his labors. In New Orleans he fared no better.

On October 10, 1857, he himself complained in a letter to his editor, István Prépost: " . . . speaking six languages, playing piano and being a good topographical draftsman, after all efforts I could never bring my existence higher up than to 25 dollars a month!"[6]

For a time he visited in Iowa, at New Buda and New Arad, the Hungarian pioneer colonies, but apparently had no taste for farming.

All this time Xántus deluded his friends and family with inventive fabrications—highly colored tales of leadership and social advancement. Unquestionably, his vivid descriptions of New Orleans and its yellow fever epidemic, of the great fire, of his encounter with the Seminoles and other Indian tribes, of life in the Middle West wilderness pioneer settlements, testify to his literary skill. But he was given to gross exaggeration. For example, the *New Orleans Daily Picayune* reported that damage due to the fire amounted to $600,000 and that forty lives had been lost. Xántus claimed the damage as adding up to $10 million and that the number of deaths totalled 270.

However, Xántus did not delude himself. In a letter dated August 1, 1858, to his mentor and protector, Spencer Fullerton Baird, the famous ornithologist who later became secretary of the Smithsonian Institution, Xántus admitted failure in all his endeavors.[7] ". . . in a moment of utmost despair and under circumstances completely beyond my control, I was forced to enter the American army . . ." he wrote.

Xántus enlisted in the army as a private in October 1855. Apparently he felt so deeply humiliated by the necessity of taking such a desperate step that he used an assumed name: Louis Vesey. Yet this act proved to be a turning point in Xántus's career. Although he enlisted in St. Louis, he was to serve at Fort Riley in Kansas. There he met Dr. William Alexander Hammond, an assistant surgeon-general who later rose to the rank of surgeon-general of the army.[8] The two men became friends.

Hammond was one of the younger officers assigned as a naturalist to several boundary surveys as well as to the Pacific Railroad Surveys.[9] He worked under the direction of Baird. In his reports of the Pacific Railroad Surveys, Baird mentioned that Hammond had been assisted at Fort Riley by an enlisted man, John Xántus (at the time known as Louis John Xántus de Vesey) who later became famous as an ornithologist. Baird gave credit to both Dr. Hammond and to Mr. J. X. Vesey. Here again, Xántus yielded to his penchant for fabrication. Although he was an enlisted private in the army and Dr. Hammond was his superior officer at Fort Riley, Xántus claimed to have led the expedition to explore the region of the Canadian River, "assisted by William Hammond."

A more amusing instance of this tendency to embroider is his report that "hundreds of miles from civilization I am sitting on a cashmere sofa, writing on a mahogany desk, using a porcelain inkstand; a bronze chandelier illuminates the red damask tent . . ." Quite a feat to live in such luxury in the heart of the virgin wilderness!

The first indications of Xántus's incipient interest in observing and collecting naturalia appeared in his letters from Chandeleur Island 19 in the Gulf of Mexico, and later from Iowa. Under the friendly eyes of Dr. Hammond and Professor Baird, Xántus made rapid strides in the development of his skill as a naturalist; recognition soon followed. His earliest collections were sent to the Philadelphia Academy of Natural Sciences which honored him on December 30, 1856, by electing him to life membership. John L. LeConte, the eminent entomologist, and Edward Hallowell, a noted collector of reptiles, were his sponsors.[10]

Baird was so favorably impressed by the quality of Xántus's collections for the Philadalphia Academy and by the items he donated to the Smithsonian Institution that he decided to use Xántus's talents in an area of great geographic importance, the natural history of which was totally unknown: the junction of the great Central Valley of California and the Coastal Range with the Sierra Nevada. Through his considerable influence, Baird arranged the transfer of Xántus to the medical department of the army where he was promoted to the grade of hospital steward (equivalent to the rank of a sergeant). In February 1857, he was stationed at Fort Tejon, California.

There now began the extensive and exhaustive correspondence between Xántus and Baird that was to last until 1864, when Xántus left America never to return. This exchange of letters is the most precise and reliable record we have of Xántus's scientific achievements; for under the influence of Baird's strict standards of precision and exactitude, Xántus's tendency to embroider and exaggerate was replaced by the responsible reportage of the conscientious naturalist. The correspondence is amply peppered with Xántus's candid views of American mores and customs, army life, race relations, and many observations on the minutiae of the life he saw around him.

Xántus remained at Fort Tejon for eighteen months, during which time he achieved exceptional skill in biological exploration. In the annual report of the Smithsonian Institution for 1858, Baird paid unstinting tribute to Xántus's contributions to natural science:

> During the year 1858 a natural history exploration commenced in 1857 has been nearly completed by Mr. Xántus, while connected with the military post at Fort Tejon, which has perhaps scarcely a parallel on our continent for extent and thoroughness, considering the fact that it was made in about 16 months by one person who was almost constantly occupied in official duties and under various discouragements. The collection of Mr. Xántus filled 24 large boxes and included nearly 2,000 birds, 200 mammals,

many hundreds of birds' nests and their eggs, and large numbers of reptiles, fishes, insects, plants, skulls, skeletons, etc., all in the highest condition of preparation and preservation, and furnishing such accurate and detailed information of the zoology and botany of Fort Tejon as we possess of but few other points in the United States. Mr. Xántus also made copious notes of the habits and characters of the species, with numerous drawings.[11]

Baird's report of 1859 was likewise highly laudatory:

Among the very important researches in the natural history of America, the explorations of Mr. John Xántus deserve particular mention . . . He has exhausted the natural history of the vicinity in the most thorough manner. All departments are fully represented in his collections . . .[12]

The eminent historian of entomology, E. O. Essig, corroborates these statements:

Because of the extensive collections made by Xántus (a large series of Coleoptera consisting of 147 species, of which 52 were new, as well as a number of new genera, as described by the eminent coleopterist John L. LeConte in 1858 and 1859; 122 species of plants, not a few of which were new species, as described by Asa Gray, the distinguished botanist), Fort Tejon is the type locality for many insects, birds, other animals and plants and has become a sort of biological shrine which has been visited by scientists from the world over.[13]

In a more recent assessment, Harry Harris declared:

The high value of Xántus's many years of . . . constantly faithful service to vertebrate science cannot be overestimated. His prolific pioneering enriched the opportunities of such broadly-visioned technicians as Baird, Cassin, Lawrence and a host of others, for a better understanding of the entire biota of the regions then but little known.[14]

In January 1859 Xántus received his long-awaited discharge from the army and left Fort Tejon for San Francisco on his way to Cape San Lucas at the tip of Baja California. He was to take up new duties as a tidal observer for the United States Coast Survey. Baird had arranged this appointment to enable Xántus to explore, if not the entire peninsula, at least the southern region and the Cape district, which, biologically, were completely unknown.

In this new post Xántus performed even more impressively than at Fort Tejon. From April 1859 to August 1861, he explored Cape San Lucas and an adjoining area extending northward about 350 miles, and sent back over sixty boxes of naturalia, "which embraced and exhausted every department of natural history, prepared and packed in a perfect manner, accompanied by numerous measurements, notes and biographies.[15]

Some eighty years later, John Steinbeck and Edward F. Ricketts explored this same territory. They wrote:

> How different it had been when John Xántus was stationed in this very place, Cape San Lucas, in the sixties . . . The first fine collection of Gulf forms came from Xántus. And we do not feel that we are injuring his reputation, but rather broadening it, by repeating a story about him. Speaking to the manager of the cannery at the Cape, we remarked on what a great man Xántus had been. Where another would have kept his tide charts and brooded and wished for the Willard Hotel, Xántus had collected animals widely and carefully. The manager said, "Oh, he was even better than that." Pointing to three little Indian children he said, "Those are Xántus's great-grandchildren," and he continued, "In the town there is a large family of Xántuses, and a few miles back in the hills you'll find a whole tribe of them." There were giants in the earth in those days.
>
> We wonder what modern biologist, worried about titles and preferment and the gossip of the Faculty Club, would have the warmth and breadth, or even the fecundity for that matter, for all his activities. He at least was one who literally did proliferate in all directions.[16]

In August 1861, the Coast Survey station was discontinued and Xántus, driven by a long-suppressed desire to see his family and homeland again, left for Hungary, where he was received with great honors. But he was also disappointed: no position commensurate with his reputation was offered him, although he was elected honorary president of the Zoological Garden at Budapest, then in the planning stage, and inaugurated as a member of the Hungarian Academy of Sciences.

In June 1862, he again departed for the United States. Shortly after his arrival in Washington, he was appointed acting assistant surgeon-general of the army. His old friend Hammond, who had become surgeon-general, arranged this. The appointment was all the more remarkable because Xántus did not have a medical degree.

But he was to hold the position for a short time only. Xántus had long aspired to a consular post and in November 1862 was named consul and assigned to duty in Manzanillo, Mexico. Baird had urged the appointment in warm letters of recommendation to the State Department.

The Pacific slope of the Sierra Madre, so rich in animal life, was also an unexplored area. Not unduly burdened with consular duties, Xántus continued to do a good deal of collecting. From March 1863 to March 1864, he sent forty-three boxes to the Smithsonian Institution.

While serving as consul, Xántus recognized Tobaz, a rebel chief, in order to protect John L. Blake, an American mine operator who had been arrested by Tobaz. In return for this favor, Tobaz promised not to molest Blake and to remit the fine he had imposed on him. The State Department, however, disapproved of Xántus's action. It dismissed him and ordered the closure of the consulate. But he was obliged to remain in Manzanillo for a time because the American government refused to pay the cost of his travel back to the United States. He even thought he would have to sell his specimens to purchase his return fare.

This proved unnecessary, for Baird sent him money for his passage. The famed naturalist, Louis Agassiz, expressed concern over Xántus's predicament.

> I am really distressed not to have a few hundred dollars at my command to relieve Xántus . . . I have made an appeal to Prof. Henry not to allow Xántus to come back before he has accomplished his task there. I might borrow to help . . .[17]

Was Agassiz's concern prompted by personal friendship as well as respect for a fellow scientist? Given Xántus's penchant for fabrication, it is difficult to say. In 1867, Xántus wrote an article for a Hungarian hunting and racing periodical entitled, "Amerikai vadaszkalandok" ("Hunting Exploits in America"), in which he said:

> Exactly fourteen years ago the mouth of the Mississippi was an exceptional Mecca for natural scientists. At that time Duke Paul Wilhelm of Württemberg, Prince Maximilian of Neuwied, Count

Mochulskii, Agassiz, Henrik Kroyer, Karl Scherzer and Moritz Wagner were there, and to make the company more fortunate, Ida Pfeiffer as well. I went in the company of Louis Agassiz. We all met in New Orleans for our common security and greater success, and in a group we traveled through part of western Louisiana and the islands of the Gulf of Mexico. Never had such a group been together in Louisiana, nor will there soon be such another. Its members represented every conceivable branch of the natural sciences, and with combined energy they descended on virgin territory in order to distribute their spoils over all parts of the world. We had world-famous entomologists, ichthyologists, herpetologists, ornithologists, geologists, botanists—in a word, everything. There was not a dilettante among us; each expertly pursued his aims with his whole body and soul.

Louis Agassiz's wife, Elizabeth C. Agassiz, in her book, *Louis Agassiz, His Life and Correspondence* (London, 1885), refers to her husband's lecture in New Orleans in the spring of 1853, but makes no mention of Xántus or of the gathering Xántus described. More importantly, in Xántus's letters to his mother from New Orleans in 1853, there is no allusion to any such meeting. Nonetheless, Agassiz's high regard for Xántus, both personally and scientifically, is unquestionable—his letters to the Smithsonian Institution about Xántus's predicament clearly demonstrate this.

On his return to the United States, Xántus was once more unemployed. His old friend, Surgeon-General Hammond, was unable to help him because he was himself in difficulties. Hammond resigned from the army in 1860 to teach anatomy at the University of Maryland. Upon the outbreak of the Civil War, he was reappointed assistant surgeon-general (May 28, 1861); less than a year later the thirty-three-year-old junior officer was named surgeon-general (April 25, 1862). He soon clashed, however, with the secretary of war, Stanton. He was tried by a court martial on charges of irregularities in the purchase of supplies, adjudged guilty, and dismissed from his post (August 1864). But in 1878 an act of Congress exonerated him of all charges and placed him on the retired list as a brigadier-general.[18]

Discouraged and in poor health, Xántus once more returned to his native Hungary. On his way he spent some time in Belgium and Holland studying zoological gardens. In 1865 he was named director of the new zoological garden in Budapest. From 1869 to 1871 he traveled in southeast Asia on a mission for the Hungarian government and, in spite of great hardships, managed to return with a valuable collection of animals and plants. He was made curator of the ethnographical section of the Hungarian National Museum. He held this post until his death in December 1894, although in his last years he deteriorated mentally.

Xántus was a strange mixture of the idealist—a naturalist of great ability and achievement, motivated by a genuine and absorbing curiosity about every creature of nature—and the hard-headed, pragmatic opportunist, who was not above resorting to questionable means in his determination to gain recognition and material reward. For example, in his eagerness to impress audiences in Hungary, Xántus claimed membership in various scientific societies. He also claimed participation in expeditions sponsored by the British Museum, the Académie des Sciences, and the New York Society of Natural Science, the last of which was nonexistent. He even insisted that he had sent collections to museums in Copenhagen, St. Petersburg, Leiden, and Munich. All this was entirely fictitious and totally unnecessary because he had already achieved full recognition for his scientific accomplishments.

Xántus had literary ambitions as well. Quite aware of the intense interest of his compatriots in everything American, he undertook to interpret the Union—the land, the people, the customs, and the life style.

He began by reporting the incidents of his daily life in a series of tender letters to his mother, and continued to supply her with colorful descriptions of his adventures in the unexplored wilderness of the American Far West. He portrayed the many Indian tribes he befriended with great sympathy and his pungent characterizations of the mid-nineteenth-century "can-do" spirit have an enduring validity. The foibles and frailties of the acquisitive society were the particular butts of his irony, and his vividly graphic portraits of San Francisco and Los Angeles are arresting. Predictably, his two books, *Letters from North America* and *Travels in Southern California*, were well received in the literary and academic circles of Budapest.

Never a man of understatement, he often overdrew his pictures and was guilty of fabrication and invention. Unselfconsciously plagiarizing published reports of government expeditions, he wove fact and fiction into the fabric of his accounts. For instance, there is some similarity between Xántus's reports of his explorations in Comanche territory and R. B. Marcy's *Exploration of the Red River of Louisiana*, 25

1852, which was published as a U.S. Senate document in 1853 and 1854. Also, Howard Stansbury's *Exploration and Survey of the Valley of the Great Salt Lake of Utah and a new Route through the Rocky Mountains* (Philadelphia, 1852) covers much of the same ground as Xántus's search for the headwaters of the Arkansas River. Xántus translated these reports into Hungarian for publication in Hungary.

Yet transcending Xántus's faults were his vivacity, his flair for dramatization, his true value as a scientist, and an enthusiasm that took the edge off his pretenses. Henry M. Madden, a historian, wrote an excellent although somewhat biased monograph on Xántus in 1940 and expanded it to book length in 1949. This is how he characterizes Xántus:

> Life in America had shown many of its facets to Xántus, and had pushed him to an eminence beyond the hope of the average immigrant of the 1850's. It had sharpened his appreciation of the shady practices by which careers could be advanced in a mid-nineteenth century America. There was in him a touch of his contemporaries Phineas Barnum and William Walker—of the charlatan and the braggart. Yet, his writings—full, graphic and vivacious—remind one of the diary of Samuel Pepys in their zeal, passion and eagerness. In his strength, as in his shortcomings, he represented both his age and his class of European immigrant.[19]

The following letters provide a picture of the western frontier that should add a good deal to the treasury of Americana.

NOTES

1. Harry Harris, "Notes on the Xántus Tradition," *Condor* 36 (1934): 191.
2. Edgar Erskine Hume, *Ornithologists of the United States Army Medical Corps: Thirty-six Biographies* (Baltimore: Johns Hopkins Press, 1942), p. 510.
3. Henry Miller Madden, *Xántus, Hungarian Naturalist in the Pioneer West* (Palo Alto: Books of the West, 1949, p. 17.
4. C. A. Macartney, *The Hapsburg Empire, 1790–1918* (New York: Macmillan Co., 1969), pp. 246–47.
5. Sándor Mocsáry, "In Memory of John Xántus," *Hungarian Academy of Science* (Budapest) 9 (1899): 232–34.
6. *Ibid.*, pp. 234–35.
7. Spencer Fullerton Baird (1823–1887), professor of natural history, Dickinson College, Carlisle, Pa., joined the Smithsonian Institution as assistant secretary in 1850 and was elected secretary in 1878. He inaugurated in America the type of field study of zoology and botany initiated by Louis Agassiz in Switzerland, and applied the Baird system of accurate ornithological description. He was the

author of may scientific publications, including *North American Reptiles* (1851) and *Catalogue of North American Mammals* (1857). A large bound volume entitled *Correspondence John Xántus* is in the archives of the Smithsonian Institution. The quote is taken from a letter to Baird from Xántus dated November 16, 1857, pp. 6–8.

8. Hume, *Ornithologists*, p. 176.
9. Pacific Railroad Surveys, "Reports of explorations and surveys to ascertain the most practicable and economical route for a railroad from the Mississippi River to the Pacific Ocean," U.S. Engineering Corps, U.S. War Department, 9 (Washington, D.C., 1855–1860).
10. Academy of Natural Sciences of Philadelphia, Proceedings, 1856, p. 327.
11. Smithsonian Institution, Annual Report, 1858, p. 51.
12. Smithsonian Institution, Annual Report, 1859, p. 69.
13. Edward Oliver Essig, *A History of Entomology* (New York: Macmillan, 1931), pp. 805–6.
14. "Notes on the Xántus Tradition," p. 200.
15. Smithsonian Institution, Annual Report, 1861, p. 58.
16. John Steinbeck and E. F. Ricketts, *Sea of Cortez* (New York: Viking Press, 1941), pp. 61–62.
17. E. C. Herber, *Correspondence between Spencer Fullerton Baird and Louis Agassiz* (Smithsonian Institute Press, 1963), pp. 178–79.
18. Hume, *Ornithologists*, pp. 176–89.
19. Madden, *Xántus, Hungarian Naturalist*, pp. 200–201.

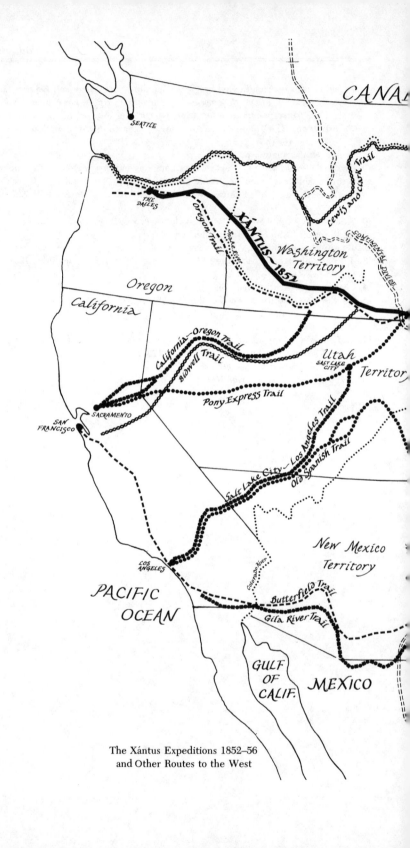

CANA[DA]

SEATTLE

THE
DALLES

Lewis and Clark Trail

Oregon Trail

Snake River

XÁNTUS ~ 1852

CONTINENTAL DIVIDE

Washington
Territory

Oregon

California

California ~ Oregon Trail

Bidwell Trail

Pony Express Trail

Utah
SALT LAKE
CITY

Territory

SAN
FRANCISCO

SACRAMENTO

Salt Lake City ~ Los Angeles Trail

Old Spanish Trail

LOS
ANGELES

New Mexico
Territory

PACIFIC
OCEAN

Colorado River

Butterfield Trail

Gila River Trail

MEXICO

GULF
OF
CALIF.

The Xántus Expeditions 1852–56
and Other Routes to the West

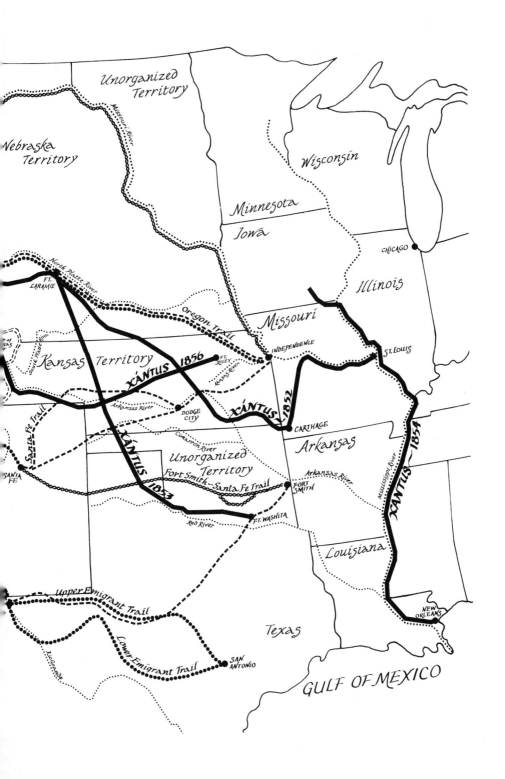

1852

On the right bank of the
Mekihaguo River in Indian territory,
December 1, 1852

Dear Brother!

As I mentioned in my last letter about three weeks ago, I was planning to travel westward. Accordingly, the following day I boarded a steamer up the Missouri River as far as Lexington, from there on horseback to Carthage, which is the last outpost inhabited by white men in the western free states. If you look carefully on a good map you'll be able to follow my wanderings.

[The town of] Carthage is only four years old and has a population close to 300. It carries on a thriving trade with the neighboring Indian tribes: in whiskey, guns and all kinds of knickknacks in exchange for buffalo, tiger, bear, puma, wolf, and beaver hides which when sent to St. Louis by water bring 200–300 percent profit.

We spent only two days in this new town in order to obtain the mules and horses needed for the trip. I also bought a handsome six-year-old gray pony and a mule with saddle for eighty-four dollars. The pony is a very fine little animal that feeds on leaves and grass and drinks water only when we ride across streams.

I almost forgot to tell you where and why I am going. A new   31 company was formed which plans to build a railroad over Indian territory from St. Louis to California.*

Engineering plans are being prepared right now in various directions to determine the most secure, advantageous and, above all, the cheapest route. I came with this expedition as a survey draftsman. My salary is two dollars a day plus travel expenses. The chief engineer advanced $100 with which—supplemented with my own money—I bought blankets, a good rifle, and the horse and mule.

All told we are sixty-four, all young men of every nationality. We have eighty-five horses and 124 mules. You can imagine what a lively time we are having.

We have ridden 150 miles westward from Carthage in four days. At night we camped in tents under open skies. We cooked, following my instructions, goulash and fish-paprika. My esteemed companions had never even heard of these dishes but now they cannot do without them. I have "magyarized" their stomachs. We had been camping on the bank of the Mekihaguo River for ten days when our work began. All day long the engineers measure. Their method should be of interest to you.

The first man advances on horseback carrying the flag, followed on horseback by others who clear the brush with scythes (axes in the woods). The engineer rides behind them with his compass and diopter, followed by two chain pullers on horseback and, bringing up the rear, another rider carries a flag. This is the way the measuring is done.

I have little to do. I make topographical drawings of the area, the mountains, valleys, woods and plains. Usually I have all this done by eight o'clock on the following morning, after which I am free for the day. Part of the company does the daily cooking, others fish, still others hunt and I join one or the other groups, but as you may well imagine I prefer hunting.

Never in my life had I imagined so much wildlife as here. In just one forest I saw antelopes, buffalo, elk and deer by the tens of thousands. En masse, they are very wild, but grazing singly or in a small group, they are approachable.

Pheasants and turkeys are so plentiful on the prairies that when you shoot at one, thousands are flushed into the air all around you; one never knows which one to aim at and often, wanting too many, one

*The Pacific Railroad of Missouri.

misses altogether. I like riding in the prairies best. They very much resemble our own beautiful, unforgettable plains. Often I hum a folksong but instead of our fata morgana, the roar of the buffalo is heard.

Sometimes I imagine being a horseman on the Hortebágy;* I want to crack my whip—instead I grab my rifle—my horse jumps when a flock of turkey takes off and I continue the hunt.

All in all I am quite content with my lot if only this mode of life could continue, but, like everything else, this too is transitory.

At the beginning, or at the very latest in the middle of January, we are returning to St. Louis because of the harshness of the winter here but for the present we have enough to do. Right now I am sitting on a cashmere sofa, writing on a mahogany desk using a porcelain inkstand; a bronze chandelier illuminates the red damask tent; my pipe is being filled by a Negro boy. Who would believe that hundreds of miles from civilization an outpost of such luxury could prevail.**

Ah!—the power of civilization! On the backs of our mules we are advancing it to where no white man has ever been before. It is like a victorious general after the battle. Truly, often I awake thinking I am in a dream from *The Thousand and One Nights*—then my Negro boy brings my tea and I am back in America and reality. But, let's light one up and continue.

Since the day before yesterday Indians have been camping all around us. They have heard that the "Land Robbers," as they call the engineers, have come. Each tribe sent its chief and delegate to negotiate the expropriation of the land which is to take place in a few days. These Indians are all handsome, strapping men. We are on Seminole (a fugitive tribe) territory and I have ample opportunity to learn about the circumstance of their lives. The men wear tight deerskin leggins adorned with thick fringes on the calves and red, blue and yellow beaded mocassins (deerskin footwear), as well as tightfitting deerskin vests. Their bare necks are decorated with yellow and red paint, as are their foreheads and the tips of the nose. The hair is shorn coxcomb style, fastened in the back with a bone hoop filled with gaudy parrot feathers. On their backs their quivers are filled with arrows; in their left hand they hold the bow.

---

*A hot, desert-like segment of the Great Hungarian Plain, famous for its horsemen and wild horses.

**See Introduction.

The women are not as well built as the men. Their sole clothing consists of pieces of red bark cloth hanging from the neck front and back, much like the garb of Hungarian monks.

The women also wear buskins embroidered with shells, but the girls go barefooted. Their hair is very beautiful, always dressed with great care and falling softly on the shoulders. Their necks are covered with beads and colibri feathers. The nose is painted blue, the lips red, and forehead yellow. Their paints are harmless because they are made of nontoxic plant juices.

They eat primarily the flesh of wild animals which they roast complete with hair and skin in hot ashes and flavor with various scented herbs. I must admit it tastes very good. They also prepare a variety of plants and wild fruits which when cooked or baked are also very tasty.

They all live in reed tents. Twenty to thirty tents are grouped close together, resembling a gypsy village. Straight across from us on the bank of the river is a village of seventeen wigwams. On several occasions the chief took me over in his canoe and with the help of an interpreter he showed and explained everything to me. The men do nothing but hunt and smoke pipes. The women do all the work. They prepare the skins, cook and bake, and when the man goes on a trip he rides while the wife follows on foot, carrying the luggage.

When the interpreter introduced me, he told the chief that I came across the great water. The chief asked, "Why?" "Because," the interpreter answered, "he was chased out of his country." Whereupon, the chief took his pipe out of his mouth, took the buskin off his right foot and offered it to me as a token of friendship, saying: "You are truly my *nekam* (good friend) because you, like ourselves, were driven off your lands. Accept this token of friendship, join us, we are powerful," and so on. We exchanged pipes and while smoking my new friend offered me a choice of his daughters in marriage. Naturally I thanked him, promising to mull over this very weighty matter.

Well, this is how matters stand now, brother, and I only regret that you are not with me as you have always been in the past when things were going well. There are times when I wish I could share my joyous moments with you. At other times I am glad that I alone have to shoulder the bitter burden of pain and privation.

This letter is addressed to you with the knowledge that its content is of more interest to you than to mother and Mali; it will

suffice if you tell them that I am in good health, contented with my lot
and kiss them for me.

I have arranged to have your letters forwarded to Carthage. Prior
to my departure I received all your letters promptly. Six of them, if I
remember correctly. Write often to this address. Every other week a
rider takes our mail to Carthage and from there a Mormon caravan
takes it to St. Louis. This is how we receive our mail, and journals, too.

I have still not received your letter from Somogyvár.

God bless you all. Your loving brother, Muki.

On the bank of the Nebraska River
[275 miles northwest of Carthage, Missouri, in Nebraska Territory*]
December 8, 1852

Dear Sister!

I believe brother Gyula [Julius] received my letter written from
the camp on the bank of the Mekihaguo River on the first of the month
and sent to Carthage on the second to be forwarded to St. Louis. In
that letter I described my travels and life here fully. In the afternoon of
the third we pulled up stakes and traveled further west. In three days
and four nights we covered 120 miles and the day before yesterday we
set up camp again on the bank of the Nebraska River where we intend
to stay for about a fortnight while the engineers survey the land in
every direction. Presently we are on the territory of the Potowatami
Indian tribe. It is very romantic. For nearly a day we traveled over a
vast flat prairie where corn, tobacco, and potatoes, both cultivated and
wild, grow among other weeds. The wild plants are by no means of the
same quality as the cultivated ones; the tobacco leaf is covered with fuzz
and is as sharp as paprika. The potato is only the size of a walnut and
tastes bitter. Cornstalks grow very tall, fourteen to sixteen feet, but
there is only one head to a stalk. The kernel is white in color and square
in shape.

The local Indians, just like the Sioux and Kansas Indians whose
territories we have crossed, cultivate large areas of land where they

---

*The Nebraska River is probably present-day Platte River in western Nebraska.

grow three different crops for their own needs. From corn they can prepare a variety of tasty dishes. Potatoes are baked in hot embers and eaten in the jacket.

The Nebraska River is about the size of the Dráva.*. The bank where our camp is set up is flat meadowland. Only here and there does one find a plantain or hickory tree. The other (western) bank is steep. Rocks eighty to 120 feet high rise directly from the river and are covered with beautiful cedar and sarsaparilla trees.

The river is teaming with a variety of fish and edible clams. The Indians claim there are crabs and turtles too but I have not seen any yet. There is a waterfall nearby where the river drops forty feet. Countless numbers of canoes swarming with Indians are all around us.

The Indians are very fond of eels prepared in the following way: The top skin is removed, then they put it on a flat stone, rolled like a strudel and slowly bake it on a charcoal fire. When cooked and sprinkled with the juice of wild lemon it tastes quite good and could pass for a gourmet dish in any fine European hotel. Trout and other fish are spit-roasted by sticking the spit in the ground around the fire, and turning it constantly until the meat is done.

Game is not as plentiful here as on the Mekihaguo, either because the Indians hunt it too often or scare it away. However, a few miles from here it is a still abundant.

Wild geese by the millions come to the river morning and night, but they are very wild and unapproachable. For this reason I amuse myself mostly with fishing. I am negotiating with the Indians for a canoe.

The Indian tribe consists of about 8,000 people. They used to live around Lake Michigan but they sold their land to the free states and moved here about sixteen years ago. There are very few among them who own guns and those who do cannot use them for lack of ammunition.

But they are proficient with the bow and arrow; it is miraculous how accurate they can be at times. From the Mekihaguo we had a young Sioux Indian guide who was barely twenty-four years old. One foggy morning he started grunting and pointing to the right and left. We looked carefully in every direction but saw nothing. Then he rode ahead

*The Dráva River originates in the Dolomites and forms the southern border of Hungary, together with Yugoslavia. In the days of the old monarchy it bordered on Croatia, near Xántus's home.

and shot ten arrows in succession. We laughed at his antics, but when we reached the hilltop we found to our amazement a dying buffalo bull struck by eight arrows. We measured the distance from where the boy aimed. It was 385 paces. You need a good rifle to shoot so accurately from such a distance.

But you are bored, sister, when I write of such matters; you must forgive me but these are the things that interest me most. Hunting is not forbidden anywhere around here and neither A nor B can shoot at or kill my dog.

To make up for my offense I shall describe how the local ladies occupy themselves and the latest style on the bank of the Nebraska River. If it varies somewhat from the fashions of Paris, it should not be surprising considering the distance of 6,400 miles.*

No one would attempt to wear here the high style coiffure or the fine boots and clothes seen at the opera. They are beyond all that here at world's end.

As is true of all savage and uncivilized peoples, women play a subordinate role—a far cry indeed from any concepts of emancipation, but perhaps this is only to insure the survival of the race.

They rise at dawn, before sunrise, set the fire and prepare breakfast, after which the men ride off to hunt. The women stretch raw skins on frames and dress them by scraping them with knives and rubbing them with stones.

From the finished skins and pelts they make clothes, belts, blankets, saddles, and knapsacks. The needle is made of the thorn of the chinquapin tree, while the thread is made of plantain fiber or sometimes also of deer guts. Women also make knives of sharpened stones, bows (of buffalo horn), arrows, and utensils. They cure meat by smoking and salting it; they cultivate the soil with stone spades and axes (tomahawks). In short they do everything, even the degrading tasks we would be embarrassed to ask our servants to do in Europe.

Infants are nursed only twice a day, morning and evening. The rest of the day, wrapped in bark cloth, they hang suspended on a tree branch in front of the wigwam door near the ever-burning fire. Yet they seem contented. I have never seen one cry.

In the evening when the men come home, the women unsaddle the horses and store away the game. Supper must be ready by this

*Xántus's figures are wrong. The distance is approximately 4,600 miles.

time. The men eat by themselves, after which the women huddled in a corner, finish the leftovers. After supper the men and women sit around the fire together. While the women sew or strip the game, the men smoke their pipes and discuss their hunting adventures and heroic deeds. Every man keeps as many wives as he can support by his hunting prowess. The more wives he has, the wealthier he is consi- dered and in this sense there is an aristocracy among the Indians. When a man wants to marry he is obliged to give the father, or in certain circumstances the brother, a horse, a cow or knick-knacks, according to an agreement that seals the bargain. Naturally not everyone has these in abundance to pay for many wives.

To take a woman against her or her parents' consent, or to violate her, is forbidden. This crime, like stealing, is without exception punished by death.

The naked culprit is tied to a stake, where, in the presence of the entire tribe, he is scalped, a horribly shocking deterrent. The bloody scalp is handed over to the plaintiff for "satisfaction." This is a very rare occurrence, however, because everyone knows what to expect as punishment for theft, robbery, murder or rape.

As to women's clothing or the local fashion, it is very simple, yet at the same time it is picturesque and showy. The women's hair is carefully braided with assorted small shells and ornamented with parrot feathers. A stork-like bird is painted in gaudy colors on both cheeks; the nose is smeared with blue paint. The neck is bare, but for a few strands of very ornate shell beads. From the front and back, knee-length bark cloth hangs open on the sides, which flutter when the wind blows, as if they wanted to fly. They are completely naked underneath, as well as from knee to ankle. Moreover, girls go barefooted.

The women, however, wear moccasins, which are finely-crafted deerskin slippers, richly decorated with beads, so that the deerskin is hardly visible. From ankle to knee they are tied with wood bark in the fashion of old Roman footwear. I heard that in winter, on the other hand, they also wear deerskin pants, which I would like very much to see, for until now I have seen them only *en negligée*.

On the nineteenth we crossed the Nebraska at a spot where the water was one to three feet deep. We climbed up the Rockies, finding solid snow everywhere on our way.

On the twenty-second we reached an eighty-mile long desert

devoid of water and vegetation. The next morning at five we began to cross the desert, and because our livestock was well cared for, we were able to drive them until evening. We stopped then for a short while, but just before sunset we were on our way again until two in the morning, when we unsaddled and freed our animals to forage as best they could.

At sunrise we departed and reached the Green River by evening. Among the natural wonders I found around the Green River, the Courthouse Rock and the Chimney Rock stood out. One resembles a round cone, and the other a tall sooty chimney. We also came upon Independence Rock, which is completely barren.

The journey until now was a difficult one and it is surprising that I did not get sick. Many of my companions were ailing, and although I was the leader of the expedition I also had to act as muleteer, cook, water- and wood-bearer; in addition, I had to do guard duty at night; despite the hardships, the dust, and the stifling stench of the surrounding steaming marshes, which nearly suffocated us, I have stayed healthy.

Like good Christians we celebrated Christmas on the shores of a large lake, but the joy of our modest celebration was soon muted by the sudden, unexpected, extremely bitter cold which put a damper on the last spark of our gaiety. We took refuge in our improvised huts, covering ourselves as best we could against the ice and cold with buffalo skins and blankets.

Here I must relate a little story. At the time I intended to return home from Bohemia, I bought in Dresden an attractive shawl as a surprise gift for Mali. But instead of taking it home I took it to London. Having little hope of returning home from there, I had two waistcoats made of it. One I wore in England, and it also served as a festive garment in Paris, Rotterdam, Amsterdam, and Brussels. I boarded the ship wearing it, but since it was completely threadbare by then, I threw it into the Atlantic Ocean. The other one I wore in America, but after the vicissitudes of all my travels it became as frayed as an old regimental flag, which no needle and thread could salvage. Now this one rests on the bottom of Lake Crifty, while its sister is swimming in the Atlantic, unless the fish have swallowed it. Thus they both suffered the fate of all earthly things.

Still, it is strange. I could not have imagined in Dresden the tremendous difference between intent and end result, whereby the shawl, instead of adorning Mali's shoulder, ended up as food for fish in the ocean and a nest for rattlesnakes, after being worn so close to my heart through so many hardships.

I have digressed quite a bit; I might soon start discussing the silkworms which spun the threads for the aforementioned scarf, so I better return to the more prosaic chronicle of my travels.

The evening of the twenty-seventh we continued in a northwesterly direction and for a long distance we encountered no vegetation and very little water. Our mules sickened from all the bad water they drank. One evening six of them were ailing.

There was no beast of burden anywhere in the entire region and the stench was almost unbearable, hence I drove them for two solid nights to reach more hospitable shores, until at last we reached the Snake River, which we crossed at once, changing our direction in order to find better grazing grounds.

Our crossing the Snake was a sight to behold. While some were trying to protect the luggage from getting soaked, others were leading the horses and mules across. The mules, frightened by the strong current, tried to swim back. After a great deal of effort we crossed.

At Fort Boyse we crossed the Lewis River on horseback without any trouble. At night we suffered much from mosquitoes.

The following letter of December 31, 1852, and the subsequent one dated January 4, 1853, offer a somewhat confused and puzzling account of a relief party led by Xántus. In a little more than a fortnight he would have covered more than 2,000 miles through virgin wilderness from Nebraska to the Cascades, which was near the Pacific Ocean. It is most likely that Xántus based his narrative on John C. Fremont's Report of the Exploring Expedition to the Rocky Mountains in the Year of 1842 and to Oregon and North California in 1843–44, U.S. Congress, Doc. 166 *(Washington, D.C.: Blair & Reeves, 1845). All the geographical locations mentioned by Xántus figure prominently in Fremont's report.*

It is quite possible that Xántus also saw a report of an expedition made by the "Astorians." In 1811 John Jacob Astor chartered the Pacific Fur Company and set up a trading post at the mouth of the Columbia River. It was named after him, Astoria. He sent two expeditions to this outpost, one by sea, and the other by land. Astor chose Wilson Price Hunt to lead the land party.

In the early spring of 1811, Hunt started out from Independence, Missouri, with sixty men. After many disasters, weary remnants of the expedition reached the Columbia just before the winter. In the summer of 1812 a small party headed by Robert Stuart set out from the Columbia to St. Louis, following the trail. They reached it in the spring of 1813. Members of the Hunt and Stuart parties were called the Astorians.

Francis Parkman's book, The California and Oregon Trail *(1849) was the first comprehensive account about the trail but it covers mostly the eastern section of it.*

Fort Laramie, on the Kansas River,
December 31, 1852

Dear Mother:

I hope you received both my letters of the first and eighth to Mali and Gyula, the first one to Gyula from the Mekihaguo River, the second from the shores of the Nebraska.

We completed our work on the Nebraska by December 16. For one thing, mapping operations were not possible on the Rocky Mountains; for another, our provisions were running low, especially tea, rice and sugar. I was ordered by the leader of the expedition to take the cattle and half the company to Fort Laramie, in order to wait there for the steamer that comes up the Mississippi with our supplies. I was also to rest the cattle and to commit to paper my rough drawings until the rest of the expedition arrived.

On December 17, I took over the command of the expedition, and by evening we left the unforgettably beautiful Nebraska River with its friendly inhabitants and went in the direction of the "South Pass." The horses and mules were running to and fro in a daze all night long.

Our passage now became very difficult; we were constantly ascending, then descending the rocky slopes.

My well-worn footwear was worthless by this time, due very likely to the unskilled job of patch and repair by its master. I therefore discarded them and traversed barefooted these rocky trails, which were further hardened by frequent showers followed by hard frosts. All this seemed to me very romantic. The beauty of nature often compensates for the inadequacy of warm clothing and footwear.

41

After crossing the Grand Round Rally, our route led through the Blue Mountains. It took us a whole day to traverse a horrible primeval forest, among giant firs, up and down precipitously steep rocks where little grass and even less water was to be found. Still everything went all right. Finally, yesterday morning we reached the mighty Columbia River. After crossing it we arrived at a place called Dalles,* where migrants on their way to California were camping.

We also camped there, but in the afternoon we continued on through the Cascade Mountains. During the night we reached the first guard huts of the fort. Here I saw and tasted my first cranberry in America.

I bought milk, cereal, flour, beef and after a fortnight of exhausting travel and privations I had my first good meal.

This morning I marched into the fort with my caravan. I handed over my credentials to the commander-in-chief (an infantry colonel), who together with his staff welcomed me most cordially and provided me with all my needs.

The steamer is expected at any hour now; that is why I started writing this letter, lest the steamer leave immediately, in which case there would be another month's delay.

Today is the last day of the year. In twenty-five minutes it will be 1853. And I don't want to miss the opportunity to wish you, Mali, and Gyula the happiest of New Years. May fate protect you all, my very dearest on this earth. Have a happier, more fortunate and therefore more contented year than the past one, which may go down as the most unlucky one in the annals of our family history.

The Almighty God be with you and bless you as I do. This is my fervent prayer.

Now it is midnight, the trumpets sound the changing of the guards . . . My lamp is burning down, I am already writing in the dark, so good night.

---

*In the state of Oregon.

1853

[Wyoming]
January 4, 1853

[Dear Mother:]

Fort Laramie is one of the fortresses built by the U.S. on Indian territory, partly to civilize the savage tribes through commerce, communication and propagation of the faith by missionaries, but also to insure the security of travel to California. However, here, hundreds of miles from civilization, communication is very limited due to the few settlements and the lack of any means of transportation.

Once a month a government steamer goes upstream on the Missouri and Kansas rivers to supply the military garrison of the various forts with ammunition, food and money. They usually tow a number of smaller boats filled with goods of all kinds to barter for furs and skins with the Indians. They also buy for cash and sell some merchandise such as knives, guns and beads to the savages.

Many merchants from Davenport and St. Louis make thousands of dollars of profit year in and year out. Presently thirteen boats arrived with the steamer *Alec Scott* and the Indians are whooping it up, up and down the river. Thousands had already arrived three or four days ago, they are camping in the open, waiting for the boats. The trading 43 started today and it is interesting to watch the colorful crowds. Many thousands of buffalo, deer, tiger, beaver, wolf, bear, fox, leopard, and other skins are piled high on the river bank; many Indian arms and clothes are bought and sold as curios.

The steamer is not going back with the mail until tomorrow night, so I have ample time to finish this letter. Next week we are heading south and, from there, to areas in the southeast where no white man has ever been before. In about a month (or possibly a little longer) we should arrive at Fort Washita on the Red River, which forms the Texas border. From there I shall be able to write again.

With today's mail I am also writing to St. Louis to have my letters forwarded to Little Rock, capital of the state of Arkansas, or to Fort Washita. I hope to get much longed-for news about dear mother.

It is not yet decided when we shall return to St. Louis—it depends on circumstances. It is possible that we might have to survey the route to the Great Salt Lake; at any rate I shall write from Fort Washita for sure.

The day before yesterday I went hunting with the commander of the fort and I had a very good time, partly because of the abundance of game and partly because of the beautiful scenery. I shot a beautiful black fox and fourteen turkeys. Tomorrow I will send the skin to St. Louis to have a winter cap made of it, which is rather rare and expensive around here.

There are deer and antelope by the thousands, but as they are very wild, one can approach them only on horseback with a large party. The day after tomorrow we shall go on an antelope hunt in the company of many local hunters on horseback. The officers promise a lot of fun.

Fort Laramie is situated on the left bank of the Kansas River* on top of a steep rock, which is reached by a road carved out of solid rock. The surrounding forests consist of red cedar, oak, plantain, sycamore, hickory palm, and sarsaparilla trees; but here and there are also a few beech, poplar and cotton trees.

The climate is healthy and invigorating, and the entire region is wildly romantic. From the powder tower of the fort there is an exceptional view of the flat meadows to the south. For about eighty miles every point of the land is visible.

---

*Xántus is confused. Fort Laramie is not on the Kansas River but at the confluence of the North Platte and Laramie Rivers in Wyoming.

I shall make a sketch of the countryside and send it to you, dear mother. Truly, I have an attractive and interesting collection of drawings by now. They are mostly landscapes of Indian territory, agricultural implements, clothing, arms, and so on. I must confess to some hesitancy in copying and sending the copies home; on the other hand, I would not risk entrusting the originals to the uncertainties of the post. They could get lost, thus depleting my collection, which I could put to good use in describing my journeys.

Three officers of the local garrison are married, so we also have ladies here; one of the artillery captains has an exceptionally beautiful and highly cultured daughter of twenty. I was very glad to be once again in the company of ladies and to be able to discuss other subjects besides the hunt, eating, cooking, and God knows what other prosaic topics.

At night we play the piano, dance, and sing. I have introduced a Hungarian parlor game involving the payment of "ransom," which greatly amused the Americans. Even the aging commander of the fort is playing it and enjoying the kissing. The wife of a major plays the harp and mandolin very well. She is a native of Mexico and comes of the best Spanish stock. She is well past thirty but still very attractive and pleasant, the mother of three young sons.

Every morning we ride with the ladies in the beautiful countryside and so I am enjoying myself more than I dared to wish or hope.

New Orleans,
March 26, 1853

Dear Mother:

I hope you have my letter of the eighth from the steamer at Memphis and the one of the sixteenth from New Orleans. For my part, as I have mentioned previously, I received no other letter than the one written the end of December. Possibly A. had sent it on to California, as I did not expect to stay here this long.

The day before yesterday I received a telegram from St. Louis; the director of the company instructed me to stay here until further notice. This morning there was a letter from him explaining the reason for his instructions. The railroad project is under discussion right now by the Congress in Washington and two other companies have applied for a permit similar to ours. The board of directors decided to suspend all activities until there is a congressional decision. Should Congress grant another company beside ours permission to build the railroad to California, we would abandon this line and instead build the road to Mexico.

The notice depressed me somewhat, because it was so unexpected, but I do believe that my company will receive the permit—we deserve it most, having done all the preliminary work. I know from experience that the opposite could also happen, as there is nothing impossible in this world, but I am prepared even for that unlikely eventuality.

The British Museum of London, the Académie des Sciences of Paris, and the Natural Science Society of New York* have sent an excellent expedition to gather for these institutions an outstanding collection of specimens of all branches of the natural sciences and also to map the areas. I have received numerous invitations from the expedition to fill this position under very advantageous conditions, which I could accept any time. I would not resign my post at the railroad, however, until its fate is decided.

If I cannot go to California, naturally I shall give up my present position and join the expedition. I no longer want to live in a cold climate if I have the choice and chance to enjoy a pleasantly moderate one. But if my company gets an exclusive permit I shall stay with it and go to California.

For once fortune favors me. The case of the railroad company will be decided by Congress in mid-April, while the scientific expedition will leave here on April 22nd. If I cannot keep my present job I have another waiting for me. Thank God I am covered.

The scientific expedition is very tempting, for they plan to collect in Mexico, Nicaragua, Costa Rica, Mosquito, Yucatan, Darien, California, Sonora, Sandwich Islands, Columbia, Caracas, Granada, Peru, Chile, Brazil, Buenos Aires or the Argentine Republic, the Juan Fernando Islands (where Robinson Crusoe stayed), Uruguay,

---

*There is no mention of any such expedition in the records of the Académie des Sciences, Paris, 1853–54, and the Natural Science Society of New York is nonexistent.

Patagonia and the Falkland Islands—in short twenty different coun-
tries and under ideal climate.*

Undoubtedly if I undertake this trip my reputation will be made,
for there are very few people in this world who would have seen and
experienced all this. It would also be financially advantageous, for I
could publish the story of this trip in any language and be well
compensated for it. Last but not least, I could be of some service to my
beloved country by enhancing the collection of the National Museum.
I would not want to miss this.

So you see, dear mother, the opportunity is very tempting and
knowing my inclination for change, don't be too surprised if in my
next letter I shall inform you that I have accepted the invitation. The
salary is very good and I could save a goodly sum even during the trip.

My only regret is that brother Gyula cannot be here, for this
would be a job well suited for him, and I would be most happy if he
could share my joy. However, nothing is decided yet. In my next letter
I shall write more about everything.

In recent days I had a very good time in the villa of my friend
Puncky. All day long we were hunting alligators and other animals. The
nights we spent dancing. The heat is dreadful here. One has to change
shirts three times a day; you hardly put one on before it sticks to you
like glue. We consume gobs of ice cream. Almost all the food is iced. It
is the local custom and I am slowly getting used to it.

New Orleans, Louisiana
April 23, 1853

Dear Mother:

Yesterday noon I arrived from Biloxi. I hope you have received
my letter written from there at the beginning of the month. The days
spent in the pleasant atmosphere of Biloxi and even more pleasant
company of my hosts will always remain a happy memory, for I am

---

*This is sheer fabrication to impress family and friends at home. In the spring of 1853
Xántus's prestige as a top-ranking naturalist-collector was still years in the future.

sorry to say that like everything else in this world, the happy days have come to an end.

I received a communication from the directors of the company in St. Louis, that Congress granted them the permit to build the railroad to California, but since the other company also received a permit our road will take an entirely different direction.

The job of cartographer projected for California is temporarily suspended, at least until new preparatory work is completed. Should this ultimately materialize, the position was definitely promised to me. Mr. O'Sullivan urges me to rush back to St. Louis to take my place in the drafting office.

A few days ago, I declined the position with the scientific expedition because the prospect of my going to California seemed assured. Since I could no longer go with the expedition, I accepted Mr. O'Sullivan's offer, not wishing recklessly to jeopardize a job with a promising future; so this afternoon I am boarding the steamboat *St. Nicholas* for St. Louis. I am going reluctantly because of the unpleasant and unhealthy climate there. When one lives on the seashore, in the shade of tall palms under the southern sky, it is difficult to move to a harsh environment. I am also in dread of the cold winter, but I hope I still may be able to go to California by the autumn or save enough to settle down here.

If I did not nurse such faint hopes I would never go to St. Louis again, but my funds are getting low, and here I would have to make a new start under difficult circumstances, which would not be the case in St. Louis.

I am definitely leaving, therefore, at five this afternoon. As soon as I arrive I shall inform you.

The Mississippi is much swollen now, due to the melting snow from the north, and because of this, I think it will take twelve days to reach St. Louis again.

Have my letters addressed and sent directly to Mr. Angelrodt in the usual manner, until you hear otherwise from me.

I have made arrangements to receive the mail from California and New Orleans fairly quickly, if you have really written there, mother dear.

The story of my journey in Indian territory is not quite finished but I expect to complete it in a few days after my arrival in St. Louis and hope to get at least $500 for it either in New York or Philadelphia. If it could be safely sent home and published in Hungarian in Pest, I would be certain to get more money for it.

New Orleans,
May 25, 1853

Dear Mother:

I did travel on the *St. Nicholas* upstream on the Mississippi. It was only in Baton Rouge, 200 miles up river, that I first found out the reason for our breakneck speed. The owner of our steamer had a $25,000 wager with the owner of another steamer on which one would reach St. Louis first.

We were moving along at a terrific speed, thirty miles per hour going up river. The captain would not stop anywhere, but instead, while in motion he loaded all kinds of combustible materials from barges waiting by prearrangement at different places. Disregarding the protestations of the passengers, he kept feeding a hellish fire with wood, coal, pitch and so on. He even had several Negroes pour palm oil into the fire, thereby increasing the speed fabulously. We spotted the other ship at Natchez, although it had started two hours ahead of us. Our captain exerted all his skill. The result was a tremendous roar as if 100 cannons were fired all at once. We saw nothing, being enveloped in hot, burning steam; another enormous roar and we found ourselves swimming in the Mississippi!

The boilers had exploded. Part of the ship blew up in the air while the understructure started to burn. Although I was hurled fifty feet in the air and then thrown into the water, I did not lose consciousness but, with miraculous presence of mind, swam toward the shore which fortunately I soon reached.

The other passengers, 480 in number, were also rescued. They were clinging to thousands of floating planks, the remnants of the ship. We were rapidly followed by the *General Scott* which picked up all of them. Only six children perished in the water and two women were so badly burned that they could hardly survive.

49

The unfortunate stokers, mostly black, were torn to pieces as were some of the other personnel.

Luckily, I sent my luggage ahead on another ship and so only a small handbag, a few shirts and such, plus my toilet articles were lost.

The *General Scott*, being overloaded with passengers, unloaded them on shore, but not on the side to which I swam. So there I was in wet clothes, alone, among the lurking alligators of the primeval forest. It was about one o'clock in the afternoon, so I thought I could walk to Natchez in good time, after drying my clothes. I did that walking on the shore in the nude. At last, at three o'clock, I put on my clothes and started walking along the left bank. It seemed that my fellow passengers on the opposite shore were heading in the same direction.

Although Natchez was only five miles away, I got lost following the river; I couldn't even find a trail. Soon I came to a sizable deep brook that emptied into the Mississippi before my very eyes. The good Lord having provided no bridge, I had to disrobe and swim across.

This act had to be repeated several times. By then I was as tired as a hunting dog and, since it was already getting dark, I climbed a tree and spent the night there, needless to say with what enjoyment. The myriads of mosquitoes disfigured me to such an extent that I hardly looked human by the time I reached Natchez next morning.

Two of my companions were there already, Mexicans, who unnoticed by me, also swam ashore, but below where I landed. They did not have to swim the brook and so reached Natchez the night of the accident.

The townsfolk are very humane and generous. They provided us generously with the necessary clothing and everything else we needed. Here I noticed that I had suffered extensive injuries. My arms and back were covered with blood.

Presently, however, I am back to normal and since the event had a fortunate end, at least for me, I am very glad to have been a participant.

Every newspaper is full of our adventure. From one of the newspapers I learned that the passengers on the other shore reached a plantation the same afternoon and dispersed to their respective destinations.

I made the acquaintance of a very likable American in Natchez. He dissuaded me from going to St. Louis and promised me everything I could wish for. He is a Counsel to the U.S. Congress, a former minister to Portugal, and one of the most honored citizens of his state. Yielding to his reasoning was not difficult, since it was exactly what I wanted.

It is a fact that I was afraid of the cold, ice, and snow of St. Louis and was glad to exchange it for a tropical climate.

For eight days I was on Mr. Marchand Soul's pleasant sugar cane plantation and after a good rest I went with him to New Orleans where, through his considerable influence, I was appointed professor of Latin, Spanish and German languages at an annual salary of $900 and lodgings.*

I didn't want to write from Mr. Soul's home because of the uncertainty of my future. I wanted to send you only good news, which thank God, I can now do. My friends, Doctor Antal Vallas and Puncky also wanted me to stay, so it is quite likely that I shall soon realize my plans of settling down.

I have spent two days at this position and I wanted to wait before I wrote, so I could do so in greater detail, and also, because I am not yet familiar with this line of activity. The joyous event induced me to abandon my previous intent and write now.

New Orleans,
August 8, 1853**

Dear Mother:

Thank God I am out of danger and in a few days I will have completely regained my strength. Yesterday for the first time I left my room and if anyone who has yellow fever can leave his room, he has

---

*There is no records of Xántus's appointment, but in a letter to Baird, Xántus wrote: "I procured an honorable support by teaching for a short time." (November 16, 1857, *Correspondence John Xántus*, Smithsonian Institution).

Also, in a letter to István Prépost, his editor in Hungary, Xántus wrote: "The Americans do not care what a person is, that is, what he does. Poverty is not shameful here. It is a misfortune, and everyone is bound to help himself as best he may. I, for instance, have been a jack-of-all-trades—a newspaper boy, sailor, store clerk, bookseller, pharmacist, piano teacher, railroad cartographer, engineer, and teacher of German, Latin and Spanish." (Sándor Mocsáry, "In Memory of János Xántus," *Hungarian Academy of Sciences* 9 [1899]: 234–35.)

**We have no record of Xántus's activities from May to August 1853.

every reason to whistle a merry tune, because he has recovered. I am fortunate, for once you have recovered from yellow fever you are immune for life.

Yellow fever is not indigenous. It was brought here by coolie Negroes from the island of Santo Domingo. The many thousands of recently arrived Irish and German immigrants unused to the climate were ready victims. Besides, they were already ill from eating too much raw fruit. The very wet summer we were having was also a contributing factor.

The plains and canals were filled with stagnant water (on account of the heat) and by the early part of June the fever was rampant, which terrified not only the city, but the entire country.

The epidemic is still spreading. Since the 1st of June until this morning, 12,475 people died in the city. Those who could flee, fled. Of course the poor immigrants, having no money, could not leave and therefore died in very large numbers.

There has been a great outcry and despair has gripped the city, because for the last five days no gravediggers could be found and the cemeteries are full of unburied caskets. Due to the terrific heat the caskets have split and the lids have been raised by the bloated corpses; the stench in that part of the city is so overpowering that residents by the thousands have left their homes and are camping in the woods on the opposite bank of the Mississippi.

The municipal authorities are offering ten dollars an hour for gravedigging, but no one is willing to risk his life. The national guard is being mobilized and they are going to force Negroes at gun point to dig graves and bury the bodies.

Since yesterday, and from now on, all the dead will have to be cremated. I was an eyewitness just now to such a scene. On the Place des Armes, 450 dead men, women, children, Negroes, mulattos, sambos, and coolies were piled in a heap. Then fish oil and tarpitch were poured on the pile and set to fire. It was a horrible sight . . . the screaming and struggle of the families left behind; people who wanted to prevent the burning were held back by the soldiers with loaded guns and fixed bayonets.

In all the market places all day long fires were raging, and in every part of the city ceaseless cannon fire can be heard, because of the decision of the Medical Society, which recommended this method to purify the air. Almost every window, door and building is jammed with black flags. All the churches are open. Priests are praying and singing all day long. On the streets hardly anything can be seen but funeral coaches and pyres. God only knows how this is going to end.

We Hungarians have all come down with the fever, but only two among us died. Nicholas Borjáthy from Bihar, and Rudolph Pálfy from Tata. However, our poor friend Nemegyei will probably die too, for he has been vomiting black for the last two days. I got by fairly easily. I was out of my head for only three days and my doctor succeeded in preventing the vomiting.

Having come to this point I must take this opportunity to tell you about an event, although I do so with reluctance because I am ashamed to write of such a disgraceful occurrence in Hungarian.

Well, as soon as I felt the symptoms of yellow fever, I sent for Dr. Kisfy, partly because I wanted to have a compatriot rather than a stranger earn the money my sickness would cost, and partly because I hoped it would cost less. I believed that a countryman would not treat an exile as he would a stranger nor profit by his misfortune. Imagine what happened. Kisfy came in, touched my forehead and felt my pulse; then he stopped in the center of the room and coldly asked, "How much will you pay if I cure you?" I nearly had a stroke at this unexpected brazenness, but because I was feeling increasingly worse and in need of help, I answered him politely. "My friend, you know very well that in such a situation it is inhuman to bargain for life, and even more so with a countryman. Rest assured that I shall compensate you to the best of my ability and with gratitude for your effort." At that he burst into a mocking laughter and, gesticulating, he said, "My friend, we are in America now. I only know sick people and not compatriots. In order to survive and practice my profession I must use the opportunity to see that I don't starve, therefore I must know for certain. If you promise in front of these gentlemen (pointing to my friends Nemegyei and Puncky) that you shall pay me fifty dollars if I cure you, and if you should die, which is also possible, I will be paid forty dollars by your estate—then I shall start your treatment, other-wise, good-bye." It was due only to our astonishment and complete surprise that Kisfy was permitted to finish his speech. He had hardly done so when my friends Nemegyei and Puncky spat in his face, slapped him right and left, and threw him out of the room. After that they brought a French doctor who cured me. When I asked how much I owed him, he replied, "My friend, if you have money to spare, pay

me what you can afford, for I am not a rich man. But if you have no
money, tell me frankly, for in that case I have to help you out with a
few dollars, knowing only too well that you are not yet able to work,
and in your weakened condition money is needed." This was said by a
stranger, a Frenchman, whom I have never seen before. Naturally I
would have given my last shirt to such a man. I paid him forty dollars.
When he counted it, he handed back half of it declaring that he would
neither ask nor accept more than twenty dollars for a case like this.

But the Kisfy episode is not finished yet. Listen to the rest of the
story, mother. Yesterday morning an agent came and handed me a bill
from Kisfy for twenty dollars for his visit. I demanded an explanation
and was told that Kisfy claimed that I called him during my sickness,
that he examined me, took my pulse, and so on, which he does not do
without compensation. He wanted twenty dollars for the time he
missed seeing other patients. Of course I kept the bill and threw the
agent out.

This morning I hired a lawyer to start a countersuit for false
claims against Kisfy in the federal court. I cannot challenge such a
greedy and arrogant Jew to a duel. I shall let you know the result. I can
predict at least a three-months sentence for Mr. Kisfy, for he is well
known for similar incidents.

New Orleans,
October 21, 1853

Dear Mother:

The land in Texas that I just took possession of is located in one of
the most scenic and romantic areas of the Guadeloupe River.* I have
already made arrangements to have a pretty cottage built on it by
spring. I shall return to Texas in May if not before, to put everything in
order, because in May I shall have to put down $315 in cash, which is
one-third of the cost.

I have thousands of plans for the best location of the house,
garden, and so on, but have not yet made a definite decision.

There are plenty of fish and game there. One evening I shot

*There is no record of this land claim.

seventeen turkeys from the giant sycamore palms alongside the river. I weighed one of them; it came to twenty-eight pounds, plucked and cleaned.

Antelope, deer, grouse, and pheasants are in such abundance that it is difficult to protect the crops from them. The region is one of the healthiest in all Texas.

When I was there in October, the oranges were ripening. In the mornings the aroma is unimaginably pleasant. There are no other trees but palms, live oak, orange, walnut, chestnut and sky-scraping oleanders with yellow, red and blue flowers; in short, my dear mother, sister and brother, if you want to see something beautiful, Texas is the place to go, the sooner the better.

My nearest neighbor (nine English miles away), a German pharmacist from Rensburg, is a highly cultured gentleman with a beautiful wife and three children. He is also a ploughman and well contented. To the west (eleven miles away), a Mexican colonel lives with his three sons. Right next to him lives an honest Swede. To the south, reside a Frenchman from Marseilles, a German from Braunschweig, and three other American families.

The nearest little town, as I mentioned, is fifteen miles away, which is easily covered on horseback in two and a half hours. There is a pharmacy, three doctors, two newspapers, and all kinds of stores, where necessities may be purchased at reasonably moderate prices, and where goods may also be sold at good prices. The road is never bad because the countryside is flat with a few hillocks here and there.

There are no heating stoves here because the last frost in Texas occurred in 1802. It was a most unusual event.

We know that Xántus stayed in New Orleans for more than a year and it is probable that he was engaged in a variety of jobs. The struggle for survival in the first years had a marked effect on Xántus's view of the society around him. This is best shown in an excerpt from a letter Xántus wrote to Baird on August 1, 1858. (Correspondence, Smithsonian Institution, pp. 2–6). *He says:*

> *We Hungarians cannot sell our capacities. I often tried to turn to my advantage my education . . . I am sorry to say, however, that nobody went further than to give me kind promises and assur-*

*ances, and I succumbed to fate, as sympathy alone never yet saved
a life. We Europeans are not like Americans, what is incidental to
the life of almost every successful American occurs but rarely to
Europeans; the American has no idea what exile and expatriation
means; he is always and everywhere at home, everybody speaks his
language, etc. and so the small caprices of fortune develop his
energies, . . . An American gentleman pressed by want adopts
whatever presents itself at the moment to provide for his necessities and never feels degraded; this principle is very honorable I
know–but still the European in face of such facts ever clings
tenaciously to his past, and like the young Spartan who stole the
fox, makes no grimace while famine eats his bowels out!*

*I had excellent introductions to several high standing Americans
when I landed in New York . . . everybody received me well, but
nobody lent his hand to build up some future for me. Although
nobody refused openly his assistance, everybody's act seemed to
say, "help yourself."*

*I once asked a gentleman . . . to help me to some standing in the
topographical bureau, or coast survey. He said he would do
anything for me but this. He never trespasses on his principle,
which is never to patronize, or protect to protect, let everybody
fight out his own happiness. This is a very respectable principle I
confess, and ought to introduced in every branch of the State
engine. But in my opinion it had been proper (to say the least) if
the General had reversed our positions and had considered my
peculiar case. How he had felt if, deprived of all his property, [he]
had been obliged to run only with naked life to a strange country,
and had received such an answer from a supposed friend!*

*All such tricks of fortune exasperated my feelings somehow, and
after several adventures, reduced at last–I enlisted in the Army,
considering [it] more honorable to serve the great Republic in any
capacity, than beg favors of people who never understood me.*

1854

New Orleans,
February 5, 1854

Dear Mother:

Today, rather yesterday, a most horrible disaster struck our town.

A steamer, *Charles Belcher*, arrived from St. Louis in the morning. It was dark and raining. To tie up at the dock, torches were lit. Due either to carelessness or clumsiness, a torch from the deck fell on the neighboring ship that had docked a few hours earlier with a load of 3,500 bales of cotton. Within a few minutes, both steamers were engulfed in flames, and in barely two hours the fire totally destroyed twenty-seven additional ships.

Due to the wind, huge piles of sugar, coffee, palm oil, 15,000 bales of cotton, and 20,000 barrels of rum, all stored on the banks of the Mississippi, were destroyed.

At this hour no one knows with certainty the extent of the loss but the general estimate is that it amounts to at least ten million dollars, not counting the 270 lives that were lost as a consequence of the disaster.*

---

*See Introduction.

Many merchants lost everything and many plantations their entire year's production. The ships, however, excepting for two, were insured and so the fire insurance companies will be the ones to suffer.

I was fortunate to escape, because I too was going to ship about $400 worth of merchandise. However, the carpenter was not ready with my packing boxes. Were it not for this circumstance, my entire winter's toil would have been laid waste.

That the catastrophe was not more extensive was due only to the fact that the wind changed. Otherwise we could have witnessed the total annihilation of our city's industry. (About 200 steamers and another 200 sea-going sailing vessels were in the harbor.)

Now, after all this horror, something more pleasant. The other day I had a visit from Samuel Ludwigh, whose name is well known at home. He has been living in Philadelphia for seventeen years where he owns a pharmacy, and is also editor of one of the best read American journals, *The Torch*. He was the one who at home was rumored to be the infamous bandit "Joe Sobri." We discussed this, and he had a good laugh over it.

He is a native of Köszeg, where his father was also a pharmacist. He mentioned the names of many families, who must be familiar to you, mother.

Ludwigh still speaks Hungarian, though poorly. His wife (a pleasant Mexican matron), his two daughters and son were also with him. Only his younger daughter speaks Hungarian; the others speak English and Spanish like natives. Ludwigh paid two dollars an hour to have her taught Hungarian, so that he would have at least one person with whom to converse in his native tongue.

The day before yesterday they left for San Juan del Ulloa in Mexico to visit his father-in-law, and he promised that he and his entire family would stay with me on his return. I can truly say I am very happy to have made his acquaintance, for a finer character and more honest person I have yet to meet. I really thought that one of Alexander Kisfaludy's bearded patriarchs was sitting before me.*

---

*Alexander Kisfaludy (1772–1844), one of the founders of the Hungarian literary renaissance and an eminent lyric poet.

Chandeleur Island in the Gulf of Mexico
June 10, 1854

Dear Mother:

Although it is only last week that I wrote you from New Orleans, I am writing again in my spare time, all the more as our hunter just brought your letter from Biloxi dated May 11.

Since all my wanderings began, this is the shortest time a letter took to reach me. The postage stamps from Kapos, Aachen, Liverpool, New York, New Orleans, and the day before yesterday Biloxi, indicate that from the shores of the Balaton* to the coast of Mexico (almost 3,600 miles) it took less than twenty-seven days for the letter to reach me, which is by all means faster delivery than, for example, the postal delivery service of Transylvania, or the Hungarian plains. It usually took eighteen days for the papers of Kolozsvár to reach me in Kapos.**

The high prices at home really surprised me. This circumstance is to America's advantage, for the poor masses of Germany, England, and France, unable to earn a living, spend their last penny to emigrate here.

Emigration was never as great as it is this summer. I just read in the papers that in the month of May alone 114 ships arrived in New Orleans from Europe with 38,000 emigrants. If this ratio is applied to our major ports in the northeast, it is simple calculation to say that in May alone our republic's working force increased by at least 300,000, and if the wars in the Crimea continue much longer, hunger and need will be even greater, and millions will emigrate.

Let them come! We have enough land for three times Europe's population, and work for millions.

That the servant problem in Hungary is an annoyance I can well understand. But here, even with good pay, one has to beg a servant to do this and that. (If you please, Madame, Miss, Sir, be so kind to do this or that.) And if she agrees to do as asked, thank you, Madame, very much obliged, and so on.

This winter I paid my servant twenty dollars a month and room

---

*Lake Balaton, the largest inland body of water in central and western Europe. Famous for its health resorts and vineyards.

**Kolozsvár, presently Cluj, Rumania. Kapos, a county in southwest Hungary, is 300 miles away.

and board, and it happened more than once that he would come into my room with his boots shined and a cigar in his mouth. "Sir, my friends invited me to a party. I am giving you notice to have your room and clothes cleaned, because I shall not be back until the morning." Naturally I answered amiably. "Very well, Patrick, have a good time."

Other times, on a rainy day, I may have wanted to send him to the post office or elsewhere—"Oh, but it's raining." "That's exactly why I don't want to go myself, Mr. Patrick. The umbrella is right there." "You don't think I would want to ruin my boots in this mud? Call a cab, then I shall go." "No, my friend, you stay at home. I have a number of things to attend to. I will go myself."

And that is exactly what happened. Patrick was sitting in the armchair smoking a cigar. At home this would seem very peculiar, but with us this is the way it is, and more so every day.* One can still get along with the newly arrived Germans, but since they do not know the language one cannot send them anywhere, and when they learn the language you may rest assured they quickly learn their rights, as well as the local customs.

Negroes one can order to do anything, but to buy a Negro costs $2,500 to 3,000, and only the very rich can afford to pay such sum for a servant.

Chambermaids, cooks, servants, and so on, go out almost every night to the theatre, to cock and bull fights, and at least once a week to a ball. On Sundays they go on excursions with their sweethearts, often inviting them for tea. The lady of the house seldom would say anything. On the contrary, she caters to them. This I have seen myself, more than once.

Last winter a rich lady in New Orleans struck the face of her maid with her palm fan for answering her improperly. The maid went to a justice of the peace at once, with a witness who corroborated her complaint, and had a warrant issued for her lady's arrest. The lady was released only by putting up $2,000 bail to assure her court appearance. A few days later judgment was issued, ordering the lady to pay $1,000 to the maid for the insult.

This would not have been too bad, for she was a wealthy woman, but all week long the newspapers were full of the details of the case,

*The story about Xántus's servant was doubtless a fabrication for home consumption.

ruining her reputation to such an extent that she was compelled to move from the city.

I could write a volume on this subject, but I think this is enough on the local servant situation.

About myself I wrote enough in my last two letters. In New Orleans I have put my affairs in order so that I could depart immediately upon my return. I went back again to Biloxi, from there I came here to Chandeleur Island Tuesday to hunt waterfowl.

Chandeleur Island is one of the smallest islands in the Gulf of Mexico, ninety-two miles southwest of Biloxi. It is eighteen miles long and between two and four miles wide. Since it has an excellent harbor, where the heaviest warships can safely anchor, the government kept it for its own use, although there are many people who would like to buy it. For this reason no one lives on the island except the lighthouse keeper. The lighthouse is situated on a cone-shaped slab of porphyry on one of the prominent peaks of the island, built to a height of 120 feet. Next to it is the lodging and garden of the keeper, who is a very decent American Puritan with an equally fine wife and two daughters. Although they invited me to stay with them, I could not accept because I hunt from three to eight in the morning so I sleep outdoors.

But after eight in the morning, when the rays of the sun begin to warm and the birds return to their hidden nests, I always go up to the lighthouse and spend the day in their company. What's more, not satisfied to admire the beautiful sunset, I allow myself to be persuaded by the beautiful sirens to watch the sunrise with them from the tower balcony.

This is truly magnificent. It would be difficult for a painter or writer to do justice to it.

Here one really sees the grandeur of nature. I could only wish to have one of those who brag of their disbelief in God to come up with me to the tower and observe the extraordinary beauty of the rising sun—to listen to the acclaim of the millions of feathery creatures, the humming of the colibris in their palm nests, the chatter of the parrots, the crowing of the pelicans, flamingos, and myriads of ibis. Here and there a shark chases after his food, while on the shore are great multitudes of shells and snails. One sees coconut, hickory, fan and other palms with their crowns stretching to the sky; and jasmin, banana and sarsaparilla groves with their thousands and thousands of colorful 61 inhabitants. Then a storm blows, and as Petöfy has put it, "The lightning plows furrows in the boiling waves."* Let the atheist tell me that all this was self-created, without a guiding spirit.

Only now do I realize the magnitude of the science of nature, and I must confess that I am truly religious, serene and content, ever since I have studied nature; for every animal, mineral, and plant fills me with wonder of the divine genius.

My duck blind is beginning to be shaky; the sun is setting and will soon disappear behind the darkening mirror-like surface of the sea; I can see the women in the lighthouse tower cleaning the mirrors and fixing the wicks for the lamps. I am going there to admire the sunset, and I had better hurry, for strange are the nights under the tropical sky.

Actually there is no evening here, because after the upper half of the sun disappears, within ten minutes there is complete darkness. It is strange, but that is the way it is.

Twilight here is known only in fiction. I have never read or heard of this before.

It is difficult to catch nocturnal butterflies because of this, and my God, there are so many, and such beautiful ones. They alight on the flowers only at sunset, and one is lucky to catch three or four among the many hundreds, for in ten minutes it is pitch dark.

It is true, the moon is shining, but not always, and not for very long, to the delight of lovers—I could say to the delight of thieves as well, but there are no thieves here, unless lovers are thieves too, in a broader sense.

I confess, I have never envied anyone more than these happy people in the lighthouse; they are so well contented.

All around, as far as the eye can see, are spread the mirror-like waters of the sea; lovely groves full of colorful, singing birds; game and fish in abundance; a splendid garden, crystal-clear spring water, an attractive house, a good piano, a well-stocked library, and the people who enjoy all this are perfect examples of kindness, honesty, friendliness, and hospitality.

Once in a while the women go shopping to the coastal cities, and on these occasions they stay for a few days to amuse themselves. It must be hard on them sometimes never to have any company. They

*The great poet and patriot of the 1848 War of Independence—the Hungarian Shelley.

vehemently deny this, but I think it must be so, if for no other reason than the exceedingly kind and truly brotherly affection and child-like joy manifested toward me.

Pipelighter,
Decatur County, State of Iowa,
August 2, 1854

Dear Mother:

It was my experience that New Orleans is one of the places in the states where money can be accumulated quickly. I decided therefore to move there, but because of the yellow fever, things were at a complete standstill. Considering this, I thought I may as well visit my friends and countrymen in New Buda, and spend the summer with them. As a rule I do not deliberate too long, so hardly had I formed the plan in the morning than by noon I had bought a horse, bridle, saddle, and so on, and the same evening at six o'clock I was on my way.

There is a much more direct route to New Buda on horseback, if one takes the steamboat from St. Louis to Burlington, but partly because I did not want to backtrack, and partly because of the hunt, and wanting to trod unexplored land, I chose this exceptionally difficult route with all its attendant privations—*sans gêne*.

The first night I traveled nonstop. It was not too bad, for here and there I could see a frame house, although six years ago only Indians lived here. The need to water the horse led me to a route which crossed the Grand River several times. There being no bridges, I naturally always had to float the horse.

It was a dark night, and after a while I had enough of the fun, for at each floating I got wet to the waist. I wanted to get out of the prairie into the woods by the morning so I could hunt, but also to protect the horse from the millions of prairie flies, which torture it, so I decided to proceed on the left bank of the river and cut straight across the prairie. I took out my compass and started out. The grass near the river was so high that I had to go on higher ground to determine my direction. I galloped until the morning on the trackless prairie without sighting a single tree.

At last around ten o'clock I noticed a black spot to the west, and 63 at twelve o'clock I reached a brook, where I set up camp, and after riding for seventeen hours, I unsaddled and rested my horse. Going for water to the brook, I shot a deer barely twenty-five steps from my camp and had delicious meals for lunch and supper. In the evening I shot two turkeys, one of which I roasted for breakfast.

On the fourth, around ten A.M., I started out again and rode all day long. About midnight I bedded down in a nice young oak forest. Having eaten nothing since the morning, I went hunting instead of going to sleep, but the darkness prevented me from shooting anything, although the turkeys flapping in the trees made plenty of noise. Finally, in the morning I shot a dozen wild pigeons, all but two of which I consumed with great appetite. The two I put in my knapsack in case I got hungry again.

The night of the fifth I continued and suspecting that I might not be too far from Trenton, having gone too far north, I turned in a westerly direction; in the morning again I was riding through the prairie, but by ten o'clock I reached the Grand River and the road. At three o'clock I arrived in Trenton.

About six years ago, shortly before gold was found in California, the first frame hut was built in Trenton, and this was on a straight line which immigrants from the East followed to California. Soon after, houses were built next to the hut, so that today Trenton has close to 400 houses, with a population of 1,200, and farmers have settled about ten miles around. I rested for two days in Trenton, or rather, I rested my horse.*

On the ninth I went on, and after two days, during which I camped in the woods. I reached a small town called Princeton on the morning of the eleventh. It was only forty-two miles to the nearest Hungarian (Francis Varga). I had a great longing to embrace my friends, so I did not tarry long at Princeton, but as soon as I cared for my horse I continued northward.

The Thompson River flows into the Grand River at Princeton and divides the land owned by the Hungarians. I rode on the bank of the river, and with childish delight I looked at the waves, which had parted me from my friends only a few hours ago. I finally reached Fairview, which incidentally consists of two miserable wooden shacks, where I crossed the southern border of the state of Iowa. This was only four

*Trenton is on the Thompson River in northern Missouri near the Iowa border.

miles from the house of Varga Feri; but because it is on the right bank of the Thompson and the flood turned the river bed marshy, on the advice of the people in Fairview, I did not dare to cross with my tired horse and rather rode four miles further north to Joe's crossing.

It was getting dark, and not knowing the trail through the thick woods, I was forced to spend the night in a crooked tree on the waterfront. In the morning I crossed the Thompson. From a distance of three miles I already could see Joe M.'s house on top of a hillock on the prairie, which he had named "Pipelighter." Within half a mile I saw him, too. He was mowing the grass for the calves and his son Theodore was milking the cows. I did not surprise them in the sense that they recognized me from the distance, but in another sense I did, because they did not dream they would be seeing me. Great was their joy. Joe even shed some tears, which he admitted was not an everyday occurrence for him.

This present property he sold to a young man from Toronto, Ernest D., who is living with him now.

Joe bought another property six miles north of here and is already building a house there, into which he plans to move in the spring. He also bought a property in the vicinity for Ignac H. (from Pécs), who is expected momentarily with his wife and children from Chicago. He left Hungary only at the end of June

Looking over the situation here keeps me very busy. Naturally, I only had half a chance to talk things over with Joe. I shall send my next letter only after I have met all the Hungarians around here, so that I can write about them in detail. In the meantime I am enclosing a small map, so that when my future letters arrive you shall be able to orient yourselves.

New Arad,
Decatur County, Iowa
October 29, 1854

Whenever I meet Anton P. I greet him with Hungarian cordiality. L. . . dy I know very well. He lived in New York a long time and later in Philadelphia, where he was a bookkeeper for a doorknob factory. At the beginning of last year (when I left St. Louis) he had just 65 gone to Constantinople. He has a fairly good knowledge of Turkish and is acquainted with the conditions there. Right now I think he is still there, although I am not sure. In America he would have had great success with the women, for he is a very handsome, charming, and well-adjusted man.

I wrote everything about Joe M., but I forgot to mention that his wife refused to follow him to this country, so he took in a little German girl who bakes, cooks, washes, milks, and so on. She is a very honest and good girl in every respect, and certainly made a gentleman of Joe, considering that for three years he had to perform all these spiritual tasks himself. Not only that, but he had to patch his shirts, underwear, jackets, and pants. He even sewed his own boots. He would have made overcoats too, but there is no need for that here, because everybody wears a blanket (whether red, blue, striped, or white) with a hole cut in the center with a knife or scissors, through which they stick their heads; they wrap themselves in it and promenade in the snow like any burgomaster in his finest mackintosh or any Roman proctor in his purple robe.

I did not stay long with Joe, for I longed to see the other compatriots. First, I visited Frank V. He lives nearest to Joe. His house is probably the nicest in the entire state. He is a true European who spent half his fortune on his comfort. He has no children, yet he is one of the most contented men, who spends his time in the company of his lovable, still youthful wife, and his friend George P.

George P. came here with U. and was among the first settlers. He also bought land like everybody else, but did not live on it long enough to put in improvements and make it tillable for a food crop. When our poor compatriots came here the countryside was a terrifying wilderness, with the nearest white man 120 miles away. There were no roads—nothing. Furthermore, the newcomers lacked sufficient knowledge for the difficult task, and so, losing patience, they were near despair.

George P. realized that all this could break up the colony of which he was one of the founders. He left his own fireside to help the others; when he himself felt dispirited, he consoled others; when the last spark of hoped died in him, he painted rosy pictures to cheer the others. When he was chilled to the bone, he covered and warmed others. He did not even have boots to put on, yet he was fixing furniture for others. While he had no bed to sleep in, he built shiny tools for them. He was starving when he planned flower gardens for the women. This was our George P. It was due only to the nobility of his soul and his self-sacrifice that our colony passed its acid test, accepted its destiny, and attained its present enviable position.

It is true that George P. still does not own anything (except the bare land) but he does not care as long as everyone around him is happy and contented.

Such a man was always my ideal, and it gives me immeasurable joy not to have found him wanting—a fine character who hates and abhors selfishness. He was just nursing U.'s family when Feri Varga and his wife arrived in the middle of the winter. As a former county official of Torontál,* quite naturally he was not used to the harsh mode of life he was to face, even though he was a man of strong will and patience. So was his wife, a person of culture, enthusiasm and good will. But who could expect them to battle nature's harshness, the cold winter, and privations, the adversity of the elements? After a few days already the new arrivals were near collapse from exhaustion. Over their despair, George P. spread his protective arms. He took care of five, six, and sometimes as many as twelve such helpless, timid or just plain lazy people, for whom he cooked, washed, kept warm, and so on, and besides that, he built their houses, too. His activity seemed beyond the limits of physical endurance; he seemed to make the impossible possible. The sick slowly recovered, reconciled themselves to their fate, and greeted the flowers of the newly arrived spring with smiles of contentment. In spite of all this, the Vargas say that this will last only as long as P. stays here with them; should he leave for any reason they would sell everything and leave Iowa. That is what George is afraid of. He sees they are happy here, as they deserve to be, so he vowed to make the sacrifice and to live and die with them as fate may will. Varga, as I said before, is a sturdy soul, completely honest, a loving husband, a humane and unselfish friend.

His wife is a devoted and ever contented person, who is not only cultured but a more learned woman than I have met anywhere. It is easy to imagine how well P., with his manly qualities and honesty, gets along with them.

At first I did not stay here long, for I wanted to see M., but some

*A county in southeast Hungary whose climate is not unlike that of the Midwest but whose land is cultivated, not virgin wilderness as in Iowa.

unexpected events there, of which I shall tell you later, called me away. I came back and I shall spend the rest of my stay with the V.'s, here in New Arad. Complying with his wife's wish, Frank named the place New Arad, under which name it can be found on the latest maps, although actually it consists only of his house, stalls, sheds, and pigsties. It is unlikely ever to become a town, at any rate not through the efforts of Frank.

Now is the time to acquaint you with the practical, or as we Europeans would say, the material side of life here. But before reading further, dear mother, look up my letters written from London, in which I explained the reasons for emigrating, and judge for yourself how good a prophet I was then.

Frank V. started from London at the end of 1851 with $2,250; the fare to the nearest town and the necessary purchases took $680; the house (with six very nice rooms) cost $800; the outbuildings $150; for $500 he bought cattle, sheeps, pigs, and so on, which left him with little more than $100. The 640 acres of land is payable only at the end of five years. Since the end of the first year he has lived in comfort; already in the second year he was able to sell a little of his produce, and now he was offered $10,000 cash for the 640 acres (120 of which are under cultivation) the house and the other buildings. To this one should add eighty heads of cattle (among them twenty bulls), 200 pigs, sixty sheep, and four horses, worth $2,000 all told.

So in three short years the $2,250 grew to at least $12,000. When V. settled here he was the first white man on the right bank of the Thompson River. Now fifty miles around there is not a parcel of land available, and within a radius of ten miles there are two steam-driven mills and four water mills, all in full use. A pharmacy and two doctors are three miles away, and only two miles away is a store where all kind of goods, including clothing, can be bought.

The stream of emigrants is endless; they travel westward in large numbers every day, buying everything in sight. V., who did not have too good a crop this season, harvested 1,100 bushels of corn, four bushels of potatoes, and 200 bushels of beans.

People almost used force to grab up the corn at sixty cents a bushel, and the price of beans is already eighty cents a bushel, and so even in a poor year, he had an income of nearly $1,000 from the crop alone. In addition to all this, cattle, hogs, wool, and so on, brought $342 from January 1 to the present. In other words, V., after three years of work, could sell out at any moment and settle in Paris or London if he wished, and live there on the interest of his capital.

They all work hard, it is true, but what else on earth could they do around here? They are working even now. They like it. They eat and sleep better than before. Mrs. V. does have a helper (there are no so-called servants here; they are called "help"), but she also works around the house herself. Since I have been here I have been in charge of the domestic department. I get up at five in the morning, cut kindling, and start the fire in the kitchen; then I fill the troughs with water and sweep the kitchen. After that I make up my bed and P.'s and sweep our rooms. I have become so thoroughly accustomed to the mechanics of all this that you would think I had been a chambermaid all my life. To tell the truth, I would not mind doing this all my life, provided every one else around me did their job.

While I am doing my work P. sweeps the yard and cuts more wood to replace what was used in the morning. Frank V. waters the calves and the horses and milks the cows. While all this is going on, the women clean their rooms and make breakfast, so that around six o'clock, when I put the broom down, P. his axe, and V. the milking pail, breakfast is waiting for us on the table. After breakfast, in the tradition of our country, we all smoke a pipe in the kitchen and then come the daily chores.

For example, we then stack the hay, for the wind blows it all over. Last week we gathered in the potatoes, and before that there was corn shucking. It has always been this way. I seldom participate in this work, for in addition to my duties as chambermaid, the lady of the house appointed me chief forester. So, after breakfast (which I forgot to mention consists of coffee, fresh butter, honey, and cold pheasant or partridge with cornbread and fresh spring water), I shoulder my rifle and go hunting. With what result? You be the judge, dear mother, for since I have been here I have shot twenty-one deer, seventy-eight turkeys, fifty-three pheasants, and a few hundred partridges and prairie hens. Right now, there are so many wild geese, ducks, swans, cranes, and other water fowl that one can hardly hear oneself talk because of the noise of their gobble and cackle.

You may well imagine, dear mother, that the cooks are not downhearted, especially when they cater to a hunter like myself. Every second or third day, however, I have a new role to play, for I am also the head fisherman around here. Whether with hook or net, I   69 catch so many fish that even the pigs are tired of them. Trout, shad, and eel are in great abundance, not only in the Thompson, but also in its tributaries.

Exactly at noon the gong sounds, and within a half an hour everyone must be at home. After lunch we smoke our pipes and have black coffee, just as at home. Then the daily work continues, in which I often participate, but more often I go riding with the lady of the house, either to the western prairies or visiting the neighboring ladies.

At six o'clock once again the bell rings for tea. By this time we are all comfortably in our dressing gowns. I relate my hunting and fishing adventures, and they talk about the potato and corn crops. Gradually, we venture further and further, until we fly across the Atlantic Ocean to Europe. We don't stop there either, but wander farther east into that corner of the old world which is our country, the one and only incomparable home for us. I gladly go with Georgy to Arad and with Frank to Temesvár, and all of us go together to Krasso, and then, at last, they all come with me to Somogy.* With what joy we start our conversational trip, but we end up heavy-hearted, realizing that only our minds partake in the trip, while we are still in our chairs in front of the steaming tea cups.

Often on such occasions our eyes fill with tears, but Georgy is present, and when he hears the sighs and senses the deepening gloom he steps forth and says, "Now, where did we leave off yesterday, oh yes . . . ," and starts to read a newspaper or maybe a half-finished story until slowly he diverts our attention.

The soul gets fresh nourishment and makes the body forget the most sacred resting place, our fatherland, and our nearest and dearest in it.

Often it is midnight when we retire. In bed, I still talk for quite a while with Georgy. We fall asleep with memories of the past and dream about the past until the sounds of the morning bring us back to reality. I go about preparing wood for kindling while Georgy chops firewood and Frank waters the calves. That is the prosaic side of life, but there is no denying that there is poetry in it too. I am writing it all

---

*Arad, Temesvár, and Krasso are towns incorporated into Rumania after World War I, heavily populated with Hungarians. Somogy is Xántus's home county in southwest Hungary.

down as it is, and you can decide where prose ends and poetry begins. I would add my comments too, but I am afraid my letter is again too long. More next time.

New Arad,
Decatur County, State of Iowa
November 28, 1854

Dear Mother:

In my last letter I wrote about my friend's Frank V.'s house and their living conditions. Now I want to make you acquainted with the famous New Buda.

If one proceeds on the left bank of the Thompson, a half-mile before reaching the little town at the bend of the river, the view from east to west is just as I have sketched it at the top of my letter.

In the background, also on the left bank behind the rising mountains is T., a hussar captain's home, and ten miles to the north is where the M.'s live. The forest, on rising ground on the right bank, opposite the town, belongs to Joe M.

The town right now consists of eight houses. The last house on the north side, standing by itself, is the post office. It is the property of a German named Kellerschön, who is also the postmaster.

The house nearest to him is the home of Thomas B., the saddlemaker. Then comes the grocery store, where all the necessities of the area are available. It is owned cooperatively by Hungarians, who alternate weekly in running the store.

There is a blacksmith, a cabinet maker, a doctor, two American leather goods stores, and all eight houses also serve as guest houses, for according to American custom they all accept paying guests.

Because of the two skin-and-leather dealers, about 300 Indian families (Potawatami, Choctaw, and Fox) are camping around the town, and conduct a lively barter trade with bison, eland, deer, bear, beaver, and racoon skins which they brought with them. The houses are of frame construction and look very nice. Next year they are planning to build a steam mill and two saw mills, also four stores, a hotel and a pharmacy. So far nothing was said about a church.

When U. still lived here the governor of the state visited, and asked, "Well, Mr. U. where are the churches?" to which the old man responded, "In Hell."

New Buda is very well located and is nice in every respect, and it is questionably due to U.'s indolence and rapacity that it did not develop further. Instead of uniting the scattered Hungarians and allotting each and every one sufficient land to settle on, from his holding of 19,000 acres, he used the concessions granted to the Hungarian cause to exploit and profiteer against his unfortunate countrymen. He subdivided the town site, printed and spread flamboyant proclamations. When the poor Hungarians came from all over to settle and carry on their craft, he offered them 150-feet-wide vacant lots, I repeat, 150-feet-wide vacant lots for $100 and no less.

This naturally created opposition, and five people planned another town site, offering the settlers all kinds of inducements. U.'s actions alienated the established settlers too, so that they could not be persuaded to open stores and engage in trade to service the newly arrived farmers who were settling here. So the town project went bankrupt. When U. left in the spring of last year, his house, the post office, was the only one on the vast town site. But as soon as he left new efforts were initiated. Georgy P. took possession of the town site, and by his untiring diligence he succeeded to the extent that today, eighteen months later, there is every hope of New Buda becoming a township after all.

One fact is sufficient to prove this: B. sold seventy-eight saddles and 213 bridles in one year. The merchants sold $1,750 worth of goods for cash, and $2,400 in barter for skins.

In the past twelve months the post office handled 950 letters and 7,000 newspapers. This is astonishing, especially to a European, because the largest town in the vicinity has eight houses, so this large volume of communication is made possible only by the farmers and the transient immigrants.

Here it is possible to make a large fortune with a small capital. Alcoholic beverages, footwear, clothing, ammunition, and so on, can be bartered for raw skins with the Indians. When these are sent to St. Louis it is possible to make 200 percent clear profit.

Every day there is one cattle dealer or another who buys cattle, hogs, sheep, and horses at high prices; in the early spring they drive them to California.

Right now a cow with calf fetches thirty to thirty-five dollars, the reason being the very rapid growth of California's population. Also, the summer drought burned the grazing land, so farmers cannot raise their own cattle but are forced to import it for gold.

Iowa is the nearest state to California (1,600 miles) and it seems destined to be a permanent cattle raising country. Hundreds and hundreds of miles of lush meadows, wonderful brooks, and dense groves are so advantageous to Iowa that it could become the exclusive cattle-raising state, not only for California, but for the future states of the Pacific coast as well.

As yet it is not on as a large scale as it should be, because (1), there are not enough cattle, and (2), transportation takes too long and is dangerous. Within five years at the most, the railroad from Davenport to San Francisco will be completed, and it will be about three miles from the most northerly Hungarian settlement. During this time the expected increase in population should provide the needed growth, and then the golden era of this land will attain its full bloom. From New York to San Francisco, from the Atlantic to the Pacific, the tremendous traffic will flow through the heart of this colony.

Tomorrow or the day after I shall continue. Until then, God be with you. Now we are going on a deer hunt; the mail leaves this evening.

If fate should allow me to see you again, the story of these four months alone would take several nights to tell.

Until now we have not been able to work because of the terrific cold, but by next month we shall surely start. Our first job is to determine the western borders of Kansas, consisting of one line from north to south. After that we shall draw parallel lines from west to east, all the way to the Missouri River, which will then form the northern and southern borders of the counties. When this is done, the north-south parallel lines will be drawn, which define the western and eastern borders, after which every county, or rather every square, will be divided into thirty-six equal size squares, or sections.

Considering that the land to be divided is close to 300 miles in length and 240 miles in width, you may well imagine how long this task will take.

Do not think for a moment that this vast area is filled with farmers. The alleged 60,000 population (probably not more than 20,000) is scattered in small communities along the Missouri River. Ten to fifteen miles west of the Missouri, the grand prairie begins, 73 where one can ride fifty to eighty or 100 miles without seeing a tree. Except for the narrow 100-feet-wide stretches along the brooks and rivers, where trees and bushes grow, grass fills the unlimited horizon. The land is buffeted by severe windstorms, which is why the climate is so cold and the winters truly terrible. There are about 25,000 Indians in the area. They belong to eight nations, each with their own language. Around us are the Kiowa and Kickapoo nations. However, more about all this in my next letter.

1855

New Buda,
Decatur County, State of Iowa
February 16, 1855

Dear Brother:

Your letter of December 19 was received yesterday evening. The mail in and out of here is still somewhat slow, because from Keokuk (where all mail is sorted and where all letters first arrive) there is only one weekly delivery to Buda, the roads being to this day only God's handiwork.

His Excellency, Mercury on horseback, stumbles toward us; nothing is more natural than that when the load is too heavy it cannot be brought at one time, so that, for example, if there are twenty-five sacks of letters and newspapers for us, the rider selects a few sacks and leaves the rest for the next rider, who does the same thing. Ultimately, when a large number of sacks accumulate, the local populace drive over in their cattle-drawn wagons and pick them up. It can happen that an expedition like this might bring as many as nineteen sacks of mail and newspapers.

Don't think, however, that it is like this everywhere in America. Nowhere in the world is there faster communication than here.

75

For example, it takes fifty-two hours for the mail to reach Keokuk from New York. (2,200 miles). In two years the railroad will be finished here, too (north of Buda), and then we will get the daily mail from Keokuk in twelve hours. From Győr it will take nineteen days to reach Buda, a distance of close to 8,000 miles.* It should be satisfactory until such a time when mail will be transported by air.

Since I live in the Union and Middle America I have been working without stop and my notes have grown into an enormous pile, but I would like to have these published only in Hungary. It is a pity, circumstances prevent me from doing this.

Would not Mr. Paul Kovács join me in a literary undertaking? He could act as my publisher at home to our mutual benefit. "Travels in the Northern and Central States of the North American Union," "Travel in North American Indian Territories," "Louisiana and Texas," "Travels in Central America," "The Gulf of Mexico and its Islands," "Utah and the Mormons," "The History of Hungarian Emigrés in North America." I could put these works into shape in short order so that they could be subjected to critical appraisal.

These works should be of great interest to the Hungarian reading public, if for no other reason than that they would be the first on the subject. I have no doubt whatever that they could bring a few thousand florins, which would put me in a position to continue my activities in the literary field.

You asked me to write about the carnival here. It is not easy, but I shall try.

In the eastern states and in the large cities in general, the celebrations differ in many respects from the European-style carnival, and also from one another. But among all these, Iowa differs most in the way tribute is paid to Miss Carnival. All over America we are called "backwoodsmen." We are the outposts of civilization, who are clearing the wilderness and consequently our celebrations can be viewed as festivities somewhere between the savage and the civilized state. I shall therefore describe the backwoodsman's Iowan carnival. Actually there are very few people here who even know the meaning of the word "carnival" as it appears in the dictionary. People here do not care about fashion and custom, but being human, they follow their natural instincts in dancing and merry-making.

---

*The distances are way off the mark. From New York to Keokuk is 1,200 miles and from Győr to New Buda, 5,000 miles.

The reason this revelry takes place at the same time as elsewhere in the world is due not to the Christian calendar but to the fact that the period between January and March is the slackest time, when people have the least work to do and the most leisure for festivities.

Dance halls or other places of amusement are nonexistent here, for they would bring no income, and in America nothing is done without a practical purpose.

Women usually initiate the dances and the men foot the bill with a kind of participatory underwriting. After it is decided where the party will take place, and there are a sufficient number of guarantors so that some profit is assured over and above the expense, the organizer of the party sets the date, and the guarantors invite their lady friends. The nature of the invitation is such that the host obligates himself to dance every dance with his guest.

The organization of the party, food, drinks, music, and so on, is the sole responsibilty of the host in whose house the party is given. On the day of the party, early in the morning, the gentlemen, dressed in their finery, ride over to their invitees for breakfast, and then set out at once to the party.

The gentleman and his lady in their gala costumes ride ahead, followed by the lady's parents, brothers, or relatives in their oxcart. The gentlemen wear their best suits, shiny boots, black pants and tails, black vests with open shirt collars (neckties are not in style here), velvet caps, and instead of capes, red ponchos.

The dancing starts at three in the afternoon in the largest room (there are usually two or three rooms in the house outside the kitchen) and on such an occasion the host moves everything out of the room into the "smokehouse," which is a characteristically American outbuilding. The musicians, without exception are two Negro fiddlers, who play somewhat like our gypsies, although they need not be as talented, because the American national dance has only twelve beats, and since Americans only dance their own dance, the Negro fiddlers play the same tune without stopping or varying it from three in the afternoon until the next morning, that is until dawn.

The horses of both ladies and gentlemen are hitched fully saddled to posts around the houses; the oxen are driven unhitched but reined in pairs into the "big lot," which is the large enclosure for cattle. The wagons stay in front of the house in the same picturesque disorder as when they arrived.

Naturally the numerous four-footed guests cannot count on the 77 hospitality of the host, least of all on his oats, hay, or corn, and so the horses, saddled and hitched to posts, and the oxen reined in pairs, are left to amuse themselves without food or drink until the next morning, often till noon, to the tune of the fiddlers.

Once the dance has started, every gentleman steps forth with his partner (the invited one) and they strut the Yankee Doodle until they are so tired that the sweat pours down their lips, ears, and fingers. At this stage the music stops for a while. The gentlemen drink whiskey and the ladies converse with each other. Then the gentlemen enter again, and Yankee Doodle starts all over. This dance much resembles the *csárdás* danced by the peasants of Somogy. The pairs jump and kick always in the same standing position.

At eight o'clock in the evening, tables are brought into the house and set; the food is brought in and served by the men, who stand behind the ladies seated at tables. The repast consists of ordinary cooked pork with carrots or potatoes, roast beef, venison, turkey (wild turkey), pheasant and partridge. Then there is a variety of puddings and apple pie (made with apples and wild plums).

When the ladies have finished their meal, they retire to another room or to the smokehouse to dress, and their places at the tables are taken by the gentlemen, who then consume the remnants. As everywhere in America, here too, meals do not last long. When a European watches a Yankee eat, he usually stays hungry, because he is so fascinated by the Yankee's table manners that while he stares all the food is gobbled up.

After dinner dancing starts up again and goes on without stopping until three or four in the morning; then everyone has something to eat and drink again, and then the dance continues until the morning, or rather until everyone drops from exhaustion.

Gloves are not in fashion anywhere in America except for work in the bitter cold, and so naturally there are many finger prints on the slim waists of the ladies, especially as they are always dressed in white. Since the American ladies love cleanliness and like to pretty up as much as any Eve in other lands, they change three, sometimes four or five, times during a party.

In the rear of the oxcart is a trunk filled with clothes and toilet articles. Very often the ladies change there *sans gêne*, usually while the gentlemen eat. After the ball the caravan returns home in the same order as it came.

Strangers would have a very hard time getting a dancing partner, for all the dancers are reserved in advance. If, however, someone is bravely determined to dance through the entire ball with one partner, he might succeed in inviting one before the ball. I myself have done this twice and did not disgrace myself.

I note that my chatter has gone beyond the normal span of a letter, so am ending for now.

1856

Xántus spent almost a year at New Buda during which time he claimed 320 acres of land under the Act of September 1841, but he never cultivated a foot of it nor did he improve it in any way (Letter from G. Pomütz, New Buda, Iowa to R. H. Musser, Brunswick, Missouri, December 16, 1859, Smithsonian Institution).

He devoted most of his time to collecting specimens near the Hungarian colony which he planned to send to the National Museum of Hungary (L. M. Wilson, "Some Hungarian Patriots in Iowa," Iowa Journal of History and Politics 11 [1913]). When his funds ran out, he moved on to St. Louis to look for a job. Ultimately, he enlisted in the army in Spetember 1855 under the assumed name of Louis Vesey.

Fort Riley, on Smokyhill River,
Kansas Territory
January 10, 1856

Dear Mother:

You will forgive me for not writing for so long when you hear this
80   brief account of my new adventures. When I wrote my last letter—if I

recall, on September 21, from St. Louis, in which I related in detail my experiences in New Buda—I had decided to obtain a position either in St. Louis or Chicago. But I had not overlooked other possible steps, so as not to be left high and dry. So, when I arrived in St. Louis, an acquaintance of mine had just received a contract from the government to survey Kansas, and he was recruiting the required personnel. I had hinted to him that he might keep open a position for me in the drafting section, but my hopes were not high; then on September 24 he charged into my room and announced that I must be on board ship within the hour, as the entire crew was there already, and they were leaving in the afternoon. I barely had time to pack my seven plum trees, and not only was I unable to say good-bye to my friends, but I could not even let them know where I had disappeared to. I read in the eastern newspapers daily advertisements like the ones enclosed, inquiring about my whereabouts. Today or tomorrow I shall write to them and set their minds at ease. I am pleased to note in the enclosed advertisement that your letter reached my friend Ventzel in Belleville. (Very likely by now there are more of them.)

I am writing to Ventzel today that he should immediately forward them, and, mother dear, please continue writing to the same address; from now on he will know how and where to send them. According to the constitution of the free states, as soon as the population of a territory reaches 60,000, it has the right to draft a constitution and use that as a basis for an application to Congress for statehood and admittance to the Union. If this constitution does not conflict with the basic structure of the Union, the territory is admitted immediately into statehood and is entitled to send its representatives to Congress. Then the central government surveys the entire territory of the new state and divides it into counties, townships and sections. The last session of Congress admitted Kansas in this way, providing that certain points in its constitution are changed and a new census is taken in the presence of federal agents. Kansas therefore is still a territory at present, but by next spring it most certainly will become a state.* The survey was begun by

---

*Xántus has the facts confused. Presumably his phrase, "constitution of the free states" means the United States Constitution. But the Constitution does not stipulate the procedure whereby a new state may be organized and admitted to the union; it merely declares that Congress has the power to admit new states, and that there are only a few restrictions on that power (Article IV, Section 3).

This procedure has been spelled out in the ordinance of July 1787, which was

three different engineering societies. Zwanziger Gottlieb (from Regensburg) has the assignment to map the western line and twenty-six counties, and I am in this area as a territorial surveyor at a salary of fifty dollars a month. This job could last from four to five years, or longer if I want it. But the salary cannot increase because fifty dollars is the scheduled pay for the job. One hundred and twenty florin would be a nice salary at home, but here it is not much because everything is more expensive.

In this wilderness, with Indians everywhere, there is as yet no means of communication, and the transportation of all necessary goods is not only laborious and expensive, but also a hazardous undertaking.

Under the circumstances, at Fort Riley a bushel of potatoes costs five dollars, and a bushel of corn flour, five dollars; one pound of tobacco, two dollars and fifty cents; 100 cigars, ten dollars; a dozen apples, one dollar; a pair of boots, ten dollars; a pair of gloves, four dollars; two pounds of coffee, one dollar; three pounds of sugar, one dollar; a dozen eggs, one dollar and fifty cents; one pound of tea, four dollars; and in general all merchandise is at this level.

Venison and fish are plentiful, but one cannot exist on them alone. One can shoot as many deer, turkey, doe, antelope, and wild buffalo as needed, but one cannot live on these all the time. We have shot so many of these animals that our tents are covered in and out with their skins four or five layers deep. Our floor is covered with buffalo skins, and so are our beds, spreads, and our couches. Inside the tent we are not cold. We are protected against freezing temperatures, although, for a whole month already the temperature has ranged between −24° to −28° Réaumur [−22° to −32° F.] and at times it was so cold that for miles the ground cracked.

To get back to the beginning of my letter, as soon as I boarded

---

adopted in essentials as U.S. policy under the new constitution of the First Congress in 1789. Here is where we find the idea that when the number of free inhabitants of the territory reaches 60,000, a constitution for a proposed new state may be written and application made to Congress for admission. Usually Congress approved without undue delay, although there had been controversies on occasion—Missouri in 1819–21, Michigan in 1836–37, for example.

Xántus was mistaken in saying that "The last session of Congress admitted Kansas...." There were two competing groups within Kansas trying to organize a state, one opposed to slavery, the other in favor of it. Each had its champions in Congress, but neither prevailed there in the 1850s. Not until 1861, after southern members no longer attended Congress, was Kansas admitted as a state—one wherein slavery was prohibited.

the boat we started, and at three in the afternoon we turned into the mouth of the Missouri with the intention of following the river to Kansas City. However, the water was so shallow that the boat ran aground many times. At last, after eight boring days, during which we worked day and night like niggers to free ourselves from the sandbars, at a small town called Arrow Rock, the captain announced that he could not go any further.

We all had to get off and cover the entire distance from Arrow Rock to Kansas City, 116 miles, on foot.

We hired coaches for our baggage but not for ourselves, because of the expense. After numerous adventures and privations at last, on October 20, we reached Kansas City.

I always wanted to write to you, mother, but during all this time I was as tired as a hound dog, and after walking all day, when we reached our night's lodging (usually under the sky next to a river or creek) I flopped on my belly and if someone would not have handed me food and drink, I would not have gotten up even for that. Arriving in Kansas City, we were so busy with shopping, packing, setting up tents, and many other tasks, that during the four days spent there we ate our meals standing up.

Finally, on October 25 we all started out in military order on horseback, armed, provided with scouts, and followed by eighteen wagons, we headed westward along the right bank of the Kansas River.

We had hardly started when a storm blew up which turned into a furious hurricane, so five miles from Kansas City we camped for the night. No one wanted to pitch the tents; we had enough to do just caring for the horses, and so we got soaked and shivered all night long.

It would take pages and pages to relate all that happened on our journey, so to be brief I just want to tell you that after continuous soaking and shivering and all kinds of hardship, on October 28 we crossed Strangers Creek at Hickory Point and within the following three weeks the Grasshopper River, Mendy Creek, Soldiers Creek, Vermillion Creek, and Rock Creek. On November 23 we reached Big Blue River, which we could not cross because of its depth. We built floats on which the horses and carriages were slowly sent across. This operation took four whole days.

At last on November 30 we arrived at Fort Riley, where the artillery and dragoon officers received us with great cordiality. On December 5 we began building our headquarters eight miles north of Fort Riley on the Smokyhill River. It consists of fourteen tents so far.

Our staff is made up of the following: one chief engineer, two assistant engineers, one surveyor, one cartographer, one clerk, four cooks, four hunters, one storekeeper, one food commissioner, two Negro apprentices, and sixty laborers—all told seventy-eight people.

Between Fort Riley and Kansas City there is postal service every fifteen days, so we receive newspapers and letters which are of vital importance here to all of us.

Mackinaw River,
Kansas
April 12, 1856

The winter is over; spring is here. The prairie and groves are green; the birds by the thousands are chattering again. On the twenty-first we picked up our tents and moved fifteen miles further up the right bank of the Mackinaw River, where our main station will most likely be for several months.

With the coming of spring, food and other supplies arrived from the east in great abundance, and we are able to buy things at tolerable prices. At the beginning of last week I was in Fort Riley and shopped for the entire summer. This way I can save my entire salary during the summer, which I could not spend in any case, for we shall be out of touch with civilization.

Until now we have been occupied with the preliminary work, but from next week on we shall start the actual surveying. During the winter I had enough time while on hunting forays to explore thoroughly the countryside and acquire considerable knowledge of the history and life style of the Indians.

Our camp is situated in one of the nicest parts of Kansas. Behind us barren hills rise higher and higher; below us chestnut, sassafras, hickory and walnut trees line the green Mackinaw River, and on the other side for many miles spreads the so-called Cedar Swamp with its numerous marshes. Here and there is a tiny lake with impassable cedar and sabal bogs in between. Far in the distance the Rocky Mountains frame this swamp and on a clear day the two highest peaks are visible: Chimney Rock, 11,450 feet, and Courthouse Rock, 10,800 feet.

The pen of a poet could not create a lovelier landscape than this
one in the midst of the wilderness; to the right on the opposite shore is

the main camp of the Kickapoo Indians with their numerous conical reed tents, from which grey smoke snakes skyward; Indian boys practice archery, canoe paddling, fishing, and so on. To the northeast in the marsh, like a large silver platter, spreads Kickapoo Lake, the waters of which are frequented by hordes of shaggy-maned buffalo. The bulls grapple with each other while the calves low for their mothers.

The Kickapoo Indian nation lived in Ohio before, but at the turn of the century they signed a treaty with the government and moved here. Later, for a number of years they were at war with the government until they were defeated. They signed a peace treaty, which, however, they again broke last year. Finally they agreed to sell their present holdings of about 600 miles to the free states, half for cash, one quarter for goods and tools, and one quarter for land in the Nebraska Territory. The money and a large part of the tools were already handed over by the government, but the Indians show no intention at all of moving. Expeditions repeatedly move against them; they fight for a while, then agree to everything until the military leave, and then ignore the agreement.

Due to these incessant wars, the Indians are so decimated that the entire nation consists of no more than 7,000 to 8,000 of the original 50,000 that left Ohio. The chief himself told me when I visited him that he would have a hard time to get 1,300 braves together for the next battle.

In many ways this Indian nation is very interesting, because they are completely savage and far, far removed from civilization. They have four main camps, which they call cities, but they are actually nothing but camps.

Their government, like that of all American Indian nations, is a controlled monarchy, headed by a king or chief who is supervised by the bravest and most respected members of a council.

The present chief is Hulat To Meyk, or Blue-Colored King. His power is greatly restricted, because the actual ruler is still Arpuika, who, although 113 years old and almost blind, is still a powerful orator in the council and as Meyk assured me, always the leader of the opposition.

The latter is inclined to honor the treaty and emigrate, or rather take possession of the new land. But Arpuika definitely wants to live and die here, as he vows every day, and plots eternal vengeance against the Yankees.

Meyk, like so many of his civilized brothers, is completely henpecked, for his sister, whose fame for beauty and wit is widespread, opposes emigration with rare eloquence, amidst constant bickering. I had the occasion to meet her a few times and can vouch that she is in many respects a remarkable woman.

Being Arpuika's faithful friend, she handles the weak and vacillating Indian king with an iron hand, and I myself am convinced, knowing the general sentiment of the nation, that had it been not for this woman, they would have departed long ago.

Around the big fire, that is at the council meeting, it is true, Smah-tiha (her name) has no voice, but there are a thousand and one ways in which she can influence those who have, and like so many other women in the world, she will sacrifice everything to achieve her goal.

Their four so-called cities are: Kaluzahatse, Hulat To Meyk's residence; Baulavetse, where Arpuika lives; then Okihoba and Smahti-ha, but almost the entire nation consists of tiny (ten to fifteen huts) camps located around the lakes of Cedar Marsh because of the hunting and fishing. Almost without exception they are so well hidden and inaccessible that sometimes one can be ten to fifteen paces from their camp and not see it. That is the reason why the military is unable to conquer them; they are so scattered. They have a good method of assembling the nation when a campaign starts against them from Fort Riley or Fort Kearney. Fires appear immediately on isolated but highly visible mountain peaks, five to six miles distant from one another over the entire territory, but when a company of dragoons gallops to any of these fires it never finds a single Indian. They vanish as if by magic, without a trace, leaving but a few smoking cedar logs.

The life style of the Kickapoo is very simple. They all plant a little corn, and sweet potatoes, but in general, they live by hunting. They do have, however, a large number of pigs. They are all good shots with bow and arrow, but most of them have a good rifle, which they handle with remarkable skill. Once when I was hunting with Meyk's younger brother, I bagged only one deer and three wolves from morning to evening, whereas he shot six deers, three boars, one wolf and one buffalo. Another time, on a wager, Meyk hit twenty-seven squirrels out of thirty shots from a distance of fifty to eighty paces.

While they excel in many things that they have learned from the white man, it is a pity that they have also acquired many of his vices,

2. *Arpuika*, original drawing by Xántus, 1856; print by Rohn, Pest, 1858.

the worst of which is drunkenness. For one bottle of whiskey, a
Kickapoo would give half his fortune, and for another bottle, all of it.

On the Pawnee River in the
interior of Kansas
June 9, 1856

Dear Mother:

You must have received my letter of the seventeenth of last
month which answered yours of April 12 and in which I enclosed a few
sketches of Indian clothing.

Our camp is still here and will be for the next few months, for the
exact survey of the various branches of rivers, creeks and marshes takes
considerable time. Gyula [Julius] would be in his element here.
Morning, noon, and night there is so much gaggle and cackle around
here that we can hardly hear each other.

Ducks of all kinds, moor-hens of splendid plumage, geese,
chicken, goosander, swans, ibis, flamingos, and pelicans inhabit this
place in huge numbers and in complete safety, for there are so many
turkeys, pheasants, partridges and deer around that no one bothers
them. The swans are an exception. We destroyed them in large
numbers to provide ourselves with eiderdown for pillows.

For awhile I was pressed into attending the sick bay but my
medical career did not last long, thank heaven, for a doctor arrived on
the fourth day and I had only seven patients all told. Two bellyaches,
three agues, and two rheumatisms. The first five I have cured, the
other two I have turned over to Dr. Revier.

At home I have never paid much attention to medical science,
but I know that a Hungarian physician would be astonished if he saw
the local prescriptions. For example, for ague the patient takes five
pills, each of which is made of: Stalagmite gambagoides, Colocynthyd,
Hydr. Subl., Extr. Jalapae. Besides this he takes fifteen grains of
sulfate of quinine hourly for four to eight hours; in other words a total of
sixty to 120 grains, and if he is constipated eleven grains of castor oil is
added.

What do the esteemed doctors of Győr think of this regimen? I
do not know what the reason may be, the climate or the more violent

3. *Smah-tiha*, original drawing by Xántus, 1856; print by Rohn, Pest, 1858.

nature of the ailments, but the patients quickly recover. I too was cured by the same medication in St. Louis in 1852. I took twenty-five grains of Hydr. Subl. or Calomel and 140 grains of Sulphas Chininae in forty-eight hours, and as you know, mother, I have not been ill since, except for the yellow fever in New Orleans which is of course a contagious disease.

Last week we went to see the Seneca Indians to hire workers. Luckily we found nine. I had an interesting adventure on that occasion. On the morning of the third day, I was riding ahead with Mr. Clelland, the wagon master, looking for a crossing over a deep creek, when I noticed on the other shore numerous antelope grazing on the meadow. This looked like the right opportunity to try out the trick whistle given to me as a gift by Indians, who use it with great success. I handed over my horse to Mr. Clelland and, armed with my rifle, waded across the creek. I stopped at the furthest tree in the tall grass and started to blow my whistle. Before long a large female separated from the herd and started to approach me. When she was within shooting range I raised my gun and took aim. Just then I heard a noise in the thicket and glanced to my right, where to my utter amazement I saw a huge panther approaching about twenty paces away. Naturally I changed my aim from the antelope and with great good fortune shot him squarely in the chest. He collapsed barely three yards from me.

Attributing this to my prowess as a hunter, I let out a yell Indian fashion. Mr. Clelland did not hear me, however, for he had ridden back to the wagons. So I also returned and brought back with me a large part of the company. As we got there, His Majesty the panther stood up and tried to saunter away, but the content of my second barrel floored him again and a few whacks with the axe put him to eternal rest.

I am convinced that the panther, hearing the whistle, approached with the pleasant expectation of having a nice antelope calf for breakfast. Luckily for me he was disappointed. Just the same, I came to the conclusion from this event that in this wilderness it is not always wise to use the trick whistle, for a panther or a bear might take it for the real thing. The panther that I shot was a large specimen of *Felis concolor*, or cougar, or puma. Its length was eleven feet five inches from the tip of his nose to the end of his tail. Its skin will make a splendid bedspread.

Once again I had the chance to observe another, to me hitherto unknown, skill of the Indians. When we arrived in the Seneca village, we hitched our horses and went to see the chief. A young boy ran in front of the house, prattling something excitedly which of course I did not understand. Right after that, four Indian women ran out of the house and, to our astonishment, jumped on our horses and rode off with lightning speed. The interpreter explained that on the other side of the hills, hardly a half mile away, a herd of many hundreds of deer was grazing. Hearing this, we too jumped into our saddles (that is, those of us whose horses were not taken by the Indian women). We were late, but still on time to see the hunt from a hilltop. It was truly magnificent.

An area of about two-and-a-half square miles was tightly packed with running deer, closely followed by the four women on horseback, whom we had no time to reach, but could follow closely enough to observe the chase. The circle around the hunters and their quarry grew smaller and smaller. The deer became confused. Many turned back, others ran to the left and right. In a few minutes one huntress after another stopped, turned around and approached us, each with a deer she had lassoed.

We cheered them loudly, but they just took it in stride as if it were an everyday event. We had, however, a great deal of trouble getting the deer home. One of them had to be killed because it balked and would not be led. The three others we managed to drive home with much difficulty. When questioned about how they would have managed to get the four deer home without our help, the women answered that with their hatchets they would have cut an improvised sled on which they would have laid the deer with their feet tied together and the horses would have pulled the sleds. I would like to have seen this operation, though I have no doubt they would have accomplished it. I still wonder, though, how could they have hitched the horses to the sleds.

The same afternoon we hunted deer with greyhounds. I consider this a most exciting and enjoyable hunt. It is a magnificent spectacle to watch two of the swiftest and most noble quadrupeds compete for life or death on the flat prairie.

One deer's life was at stake; the other, its pride challenged, displayed that high degree of enthusiasm which is the mark of the noble animal.

It is truly beautiful to see them exert all the strength with which

God has endowed them, and even surpass it, as one after the other sails through the air. They run so fast that their feet are invisible.

We caught another four deer in this manner, but we chased two antelope without success.

Elk Creek,
southwestern Kansas,
June 30, 1856

Dear Mother:

On June 10 two survey parties sent by President Franklin Pierce joined us again. The one under the command of MacGilnes took over our position, and we were ordered to the southern line to reconnoiter Comanche territory and to survey the rivers, creeks, and tributaries of the Canadian River. The newly arrived second party took a position between us and the first group, mainly to maintain liaison.

On June 12 we started out to take up our new position with twelve wagons and sixty-five mules, not including our riding horses; eight oxen pulled each wagon loaded with 4,500 pounds of freight.

We were to cover a distance of 130 miles in five days, calculated at the rate of thirty miles a day. But a journey took much longer, due to the countless bodies of water, creeks and rivers over which manageable crossings had to be searched for and found, or, with the help of pickaxes, hacked, in order to proceed. All this took considerable time. Often there was no prospect of finding firewood, and if the caravan happened to be in a place where cooking was possible, it just stopped there, even though it may have been no further than five to six miles from the last camp site.

The first day we traveled through wooded country and covered only eight miles, because we had constantly to hack a path. Toward evening we reached the end of the forest, where we set up camp next to a creek, which we named Jefferson Creek. It was about twenty-five yards wide where we crossed it next day, when we advanced twenty-five miles over richly green meadowland which will be eminently suitable for agriculture some day.

On June 14, advancing thirty miles, we arrived at the Big Washita River where it was about 400 feet wide and three to four feet deep. We immediately rode over it and settled down on the shore near a few poplars, to wait for the wagons.

The Washita is a very rapid-flowing, twisting river. It is turbid because of the red clay it carries. Our wagons did not arrive that night nor the following morning, which caused us considerable anxiety, for the current was becoming increasingly swift and we were afraid that if they were further delayed, they would not be able to cross it. After a short consultation I swam over with three mules (by this time the river was five to six feet deep) to urge on the wagons. After a ride of about ten miles I found them.

The previous day a big shower flooded the meadows, so that the wagons advanced with great difficulty. The axles on many had broken, and repairing them caused much delay; nevertheless, we reached the river on the sixteenth, where, to our great relief, we found it was once more receding; taking advantage of this, we immediately drove the wagons across and the same day advanced another fifteen miles. On the seventeenth, we reached the Dupont River, after traveling twenty-eight miles. The river is about 300 feet wide at this point, and although it is no deeper than two feet, the shifting sandy bottom gave us a lot of trouble when we crossed it on the morning of the eighteenth. If the animals and wagons stopped even for a second they would sink knee- and axle-deep into the sand, and it took a tremendous effort to pull them out. We had to unload several wagons and carry their contents on our back. It was nearly midnight by the time we completed the crossing, because, aside from the aforementioned obstacles, we also had to hack and chop away to level the high bank in order to ride over it. In spite of enormous physical effort, we could complete the operation only by hitching twenty to twenty-four oxen to each wagon. The exertion exhausted men and beast so much that we spent the entire day of the nineteenth just resting.

At last on the night of the twentieth we arrived safely at Elk Creek; this being our destination, we devoted the whole day of the twenty-first to finding a suitable place to set up camp. We did this on the twenty-second at a northerly latitude of 37°50′ and westerly longitude of 99°33′ on a fork of the Elk formed by its northern and eastern branches.

The Elk Creek at our camp is about 180 feet wide and ten to twelve feet deep and is teeming with an immense number of fish, turtle and crab. Wild hens, partridges, deer, buffalo and antelope are also very numerous, but there are few turkeys because there are no woods nearby.

Until now we have been occupied only with setting up camp, calculating longitude and latitude, meteorological and magnetic observations, but by next week we will really get down to work. How long we will stay here is still uncertain; possibly a year, but it may be only a few months. Everything here depends on the topographical nature of the area. Nothing can be decided in advance, for we know nothing about the territory.

Xántus was a member of a military detachment assigned to construct a wagon road from Fort Leavenworth to Bridger's Pass, Wyoming. The officer in command was Lieutenant Francis T. Bryan, who supervised the building of roads in the Kansas and Nebraska Territories from 1855 to 1858. Xántus may well have been assigned to lead the expedition he describes.

Elk Creek,
Kansas Territory
September 14, 1856

Dear Mother:

It is only a few hours ago that I dismounted, after riding nearly 700 miles. You can imagine how tired and numb I am, yet I do not want to miss the opportunity to let you know how I am—all the more so, as my last letters home were written on June 30 and July 5.

The post is leaving for Riley within half an hour. This time I only want to inform you that neither hardships nor adversity nor climate could break my sturdy and vigorous health.

Since my last letter I was entrusted with an expedition to conquer the Canadian River and to map all its northern tributaries.

I started my expedition on July 10 and after many difficulties returned safely tonight. Many had given us up for lost. Following the southern border of Kansas from east to west I have traveled over terrain no white man ever visited before. I have discovered many small rivers and creeks unknown to geography and came upon gigantic gypsum and coal deposits.

At present, time and space does not permit me to write in detail of this important journey, but in the next post I shall send excerpts from my diary which are of general interest.

Your letter of July 8, mother dear—which was awaiting me for quite a while—was a very pleasant surprise, and so was another piece of pleasing news—my salary was raised to $65 a month from July 1 on. It is the equivalent of about 150 florins.

You are quite right, mother—almost as if you guessed my plans—the farther and farther I travel, the closer I shall get to where I started from—home. If I can save enough money to carry out my plans, it is my intention to go to California, Sandwich Islands, Japan, China, East Indies, and Constantinople, perhaps next year. This last stop will not be far from Győr compared to the present.

In order not to send my letters half empty, I enclose a few copies of Indian weapons. The originals are all in my possession, intended for the Hungarian National Museum. They are mostly Kickapoo weapons, but a few are Comanche and Kiowa. There are also some Delaware curios among them. The illustration marked with X is a Comanche drum which is tied to the arm from the back and struck from the front with the fists. The hanging fringes represent the hairlocks of slain enemies. The two carvings above the drums are stone pipes.

This long letter is dated September 26, 1856, but it goes back to recite, in diary form, the events between June 30 and September.

Elk Creek,
Kansas Territory
September 26, 1856

Dear Mother:

To keep my promise in my letter of last week, the thirteenth of this month, I shall relate some of the highlights of my expedition, which I think will be of interest to you.

Order was received from the federal government for the topographical examination of the entire southern line of Kansas all the way
to the southwestern corner, and the chief engineer honored me with
this important task. After completing the preliminary work, I left on
the morning of July 10 in my usual good spirits for this long and hazardous trip. My company consisted of one assistant engineer, one clerk,
four oxcarts, and two wagons drawn by six mule teams. The wagons
were loaded with provisions, tools and various necessities. All told we
were thirty-two people.

At first it was my intention to send you only an outline of my
travels, but right now, having a little free time, I have decided to
include excerpts from my diary. This will serve the purpose of
acquainting you with my ideas, my line of thinking, and the circumstances which surround an expedition of this kind. So, dear
mother, sit back in comfort in the rear wagon together with Mali. I will
ride beside you telling about the trip, while we slowly proceed.

On the morning of July 10 we crossed Elk Creek without any
trouble and traveled almost the entire day in a straight westerly
direction. Needless to say it was an unbeaten path. As we crossed the
Elk, our compass was our only guide until we reached Sweet Creek.
The country on both banks of the creek is a high plateau with rolling
hills of powdery limestone. It was very cold, in the preceding few days
considering the season. The temperature dropped from 97° to 68°
Fahrenheit. I have never experienced this before under this latitude.
Wherever I traveled until now over the barren American prairie
during the summer, usually around eight in the morning, a gentle
breeze always blew, which grew in intensity until the evening. By
midnight it would disappear completely. Ordinarily it blows hardest at
three in the afternoon. This wind, which comes from the south, starts
and stops with the same punctuality as the ocean winds over the
Atlantic coast, and probably this circumstance is responsible for the
opinion that it originates in the Gulf of Mexico. These cooling and
biting winds temper the heat of the burning rays of the sun, which
otherwise would be unbearable. In the evening I calculated the
latitude of this place. The result was 35°26′13″.

July 11. At three in the morning we forded Sweet Creek,
climbed the bank and once again headed westward. We had gone
about eight miles when we discovered numerous Indian footprints,
although no Indians live around here. Since we have not seen their
tents anywhere, it was the opinion of my Indian interpreter that very

4. *Indian Artifacts*, original drawing by Xántus, 1856; print by Rohn, Pest, 1858.

likely the Kiowas had camped here in preparation for a battle with the Comanches.

He continued, saying that in the afternoon he had noticed four Indian outposts on a high hillock. Upon seeing him the Indians rode off with great speed. I must admit this worried me, for their unwillingness to communicate with us made me suspect that they wanted to attack us. After lengthy consideration I decided that whatever fate may bring, friend or foe, I would meet it with my customary preparation.

My usual method of setting up camp (when I can find the right place, which I do most of the time) is to settle near the bend of a river or creek that forms a half circle. The tents and wagons close the half circle from one end of the water to the other, leaving sufficient space for the expedition. In this way, we are usually protected from the front and two sides by the water, while in the rear the tents and wagons guard us from a surprise attack.

As soon as I arrive at a camp site the wagons are unhitched, the horses unsaddled, and all the animals are set out to graze as close to the camp as possible, under the supervision of the drivers, who are armed to the teeth.

We ordinarily start our daily journey at three in the morning and usually by eleven or twelve we have our camp set up. This way the livestock can graze until sunset, at which time they are driven into the closed circle, where the horses and mules are hitched on long lines and the oxen are chained to the wagons. At sunset guards are set up, who circulate around the camp the entire night, always keeping an eye on the livestock.

Many believe that the oxen would serve us better and stay in prime condition on a trip like this if they were allowed to graze in the morning before they are hitched. Such an arrangement would necessitate traveling in the frightful heat of the day. It is also claimed that oxen graze only at certain times of day and that they spend the remainder sleeping and resting. If they are not permitted to do this they deteriorate. I hold a completely opposite view, however, based on long experience, and can state that oxen will accommodate themselves to any circumstance as to the time of work and rest. It is true that if their schedule of working and feeding at a fixed time is changed for a few days they will suffer, but very quickly they will get used to the change and work and feed just as well as before. This is a fact.

If one starts early, as I do, the daily journey ends before the great heat starts, and as I mentioned before, if the cattle graze in the morning before the start, one must travel during the middle of the day. The animals, especially the oxen, suffer unbearably from the heat, insects and ticks, so it is obvious that they are better off under my regimen.

We are traveling through a high rolling prairie. Here and there are sugarloaf-shaped granite cones with such steep peaks that it is impossible to climb them. I attempted it several times, but once I tumbled down and nearly smashed my nose, so reluctantly I gave up the attempt. The soil is almost exclusively gray sand; the vegetation consists of stunted roots and cacti, laced here and there with dwarf oak bushes.

The stream which we follow runs parallel to the Red River and offers us comfortable camp sites almost everywhere. Judged by the many camp sites and chopped-down stumps, I reasoned that this stream must be a favorite hunting ground of the Kiowa and Comanche Indians. It is most probable that they could be found here during the season when the buffalo wander from north to south or vice versa. The Indian footprints that we saw today were leading southward and, since they were without their families, our interpreters surmised that they were a band of mule rustlers on their way to Mexico. I regret that I did not meet them, for it is possible that I may have dissuaded them.

They will see our traces, however, and if they are friendly they will surely look for us. If they don't, I shall dispatch an Indian [Xántus's Delaware scout] to search for their camp and find out what their intentions are, although this might lead to a lot of trouble, as the Delaware are traditional enemies [of the Prairie Indians] and fear meeting them. My scout stoutly maintains that he would not be afraid of three or four of them, but would prefer not to meet more. I told him, if he should meet them, to invite them for a talk with me. "Vey well," he answered, "but what if they skin me alive? Should I still deliver the message?"

This same Delaware lived for a long time among the prairie Indians and speaks and understands their dialect perfectly. When he reads their prints he can tell at once to what nation they belong, with how many horses and mules they travel, whether their wives and children are with them, and if they are on the warpath or a hunting trip. He could even tell how fresh the traces are (with a few hours difference) and many other small details, which are of great importance on such an expedition.

This quality, although it seems to be inborn and instinctive, is exclusively inherent in the American Indian, for I have never seen a white man possess this kind of accurate judgment. For example, today as we encountered many Indian prints, one of the Delawares glanced at some, removed a few blades of weed, and announced that the prints were two days old. We were convinced that they were fresh prints. Later our scouts confirmed that the Indian was right.

On another occasion when I was riding on the prairie, I noticed many footprints on a sandy hillock. They appeared to be bearprints, the toes and heels clearly outlined. It is very unusual to find bearprints in that area, and when I called this to the attention of the Kickapoo who was with me, he smilingly pointed to the many individual flower leaves dangling over the prints and then remarked that when the wind blows, the shaking of the leaves removes the fine sand from the coarse gravel on the soil, thus creating the image of bearprints. This explanation thoroughly convinced me of my error. It was simple, plausible, and sensible. I am certain that the solution of this problem would have caused definite headaches to any naturalist from Oxford or Jena.

Many of these Delaware unquestionably could be very useful were they inducted into the Union army of the west, since they know the language, character, and customs of the prairie tribes perfectly, as well as the terrain. Their ability to track human footprints is not possible to teach to white soldiers. Several times I have sent out a half dozen wagon drivers to search for cattle lost on the prairie and after an all-day search they could not find them. At such times I would send an Indian who, after circling the camp, found a clue which he would then follow until he found the missing cattle. One can well imagine that on a journey such as mine this service is invaluable.

July 12. Today we followed the westward course of Sweet Creek for a few miles from our present station, when both we and the creek turned north. The general aspect of the terrain has not changed, although it is not as sandy nor as tiring as it was yesterday. In the morning a long, bluish mountain range appeared on the horizon at a distance of about fifty miles toward the northeast. It seems to have a great many high peaks and probably belongs to the so-called "Llano Estacado" mountains.

We found evidence at our camp site that a large band of Indians camped at the same spot about ten days ago. The tracks of many horses and mules were visible all around and the tall grass was trampled in all directions.

The Indians' tents had been pitched in the very place we were camping, and judging by the number of tent holes, my interpreter concluded that they were Kiowas. Upon questioning the interpreter about how he arrived at this conclusion with such certainty, he explained that the Kiowas always dig a fireplace two-and-a-half feet in diameter, unlike other prairie Indians, who build much wider ones. He said also that the Kiowas always spread their tents on five poles.

Not far from us on the creek where we camped there was a beaver colony. I don't think I exaggerate if I state that there is no animal on the face of the earth about which travelers and naturalists have written more than the beaver. Many people rate them equal to the human species from the standpoint of intelligence and ingenuity. Among other things it is written about them that they build large, multistoried houses in the water, which are divided into rooms and chambers and plastered with mud as smoothly as if a first class plasterer had done the work, and that they drive stakes of five to six inches in diameter into the bottom as solidly as if a miller's bull had driven them in. They are capable of many more miraculous deeds which to my mind are difficult to prove by credible witnesses. It is a fact, however, that setting aside some of the questionable claims, there is plenty to admire in the beaver's accomplishments. For example, in examining the dam that beavers have built across the creek right here, near us, I was filled with great astonishment and pleasure, noting the admirable touch, inexhaustible patience, and exemplary diligence with which they carry out their work. In the choice and construction of the dam, undeniably something higher than animal instinct guides them, for the placement of the dam was done with hydrostatic precision and with such clever calculation of the flow of the current that it could put to shame any famous Swiss mill builder. They picked a spot where the water narrows between two high banks which are high enough to support a dam five to six feet high. Then they picked poplars twenty-two inches in diameter which, facing each other on opposite banks slanted over the water. These were cut at the base by the beavers' teeth (the marks were unmistakably visible on the trunks) and floated down the water to the chosen spot where the thick ends were tied to the near bank, and the leafy ends to the opposite bank and coupled in the center to another tree.

This then formed the foundation on which the earthen dams were built—just like the method used by Hungarian millers when they 101 build a mill dam, that is, one layer of reeds, one layer of earth and so forth. The slim end of the reed is turned downward alongside the flow of the water. When the dam reaches sufficient height, about two feet, it is compacted with hard soil mixed with turf, except in the center, where a square opening is left for the surplus water to flow through when the creek swells to such height that the dam may be endangered. After a minute examination of the structure built by these intelligent quadrupeds, I came to the conclusion that probably the first reed dam builder learned the technique of this hydrostatic construction from the beaver. They are exactly alike in every detail. I hid for quite a while, trying to catch a glimpse of these workers, but I had no luck in observing even one of them. I do believe that the reason is they are not too happy with all the noise coming from our camp and consider it wiser to stay in their underwater dwellings until the uninvited guests depart.

About a half-mile further I found another dam in the process of being built. Two trees on both banks were already chopped down, but not being able to drop them in the water according to their plan, they stopped further work on it.

Since Sweet Creek turns due north here, I am forced to leave it and lead my caravan in a westerly direction; it is a hardship because the creek offered fresh water, good grazing, and as much comfort as one can reasonably expect in this wilderness.

July 13. Leaving the expedition at the camp on Sweet Creek, I embarked on an excursion with three others to the point where the Flag River joins the Arkansas River which according to my calculations, was only six miles to the the southwest. The Arkansas was 287 feet wide where we came on it, but only one-fifth of its bed was covered with water, which greatly surprised me. Tasting the water I found nothing acidy in it. Riding for a distance of about a mile on the river bank, I found that the good water we had been drinking came from the Flag River. (It is common knowledge that the Arkansas is salty.) I was even more surprised to find that just above the mouth of the Flag River the bed of the Arkansas was completely dry. Not one drop of water was visible, even though the river bed was 200 feet wide. The entire sandy bottom was shiny with white spots, which on closer inspection proved to be pure salt. Here as in many other places the Arkansas has three separate beds which surround the river banks like so many earthen steps. The first line rises about eight feet above the bed, the second

5. *The Source of the Arkansas River*, original drawing by Xántus, August 1, 1856; print by Rohn, Pest, 1858.

fifteen to twenty feet and the third, which dams off the river valley like a vertical fence, is fifty to 100 feet high. The first bed is exposed to floods, as it is only eighty to 200 feet wide; the second, however, is never covered with water, having a width of 1,400 to 2,000 feet. The banks of the third bed skirt the high prairie. We observed that this area, too, is covered with gray sand mixed with some granite. All day long we saw a range of high rocky peaks which, as I mentioned before, form a branch of the Llano Estacado. Here we found the tracks of a large group of Indians which traveled alongside the river, just ahead of our party.

When we rode back to the camp, we came upon two splendid ice-cold springs surrounded by lovely turf, and not far from it abundant mesquite grass (*Algarobia glandulosa*), a circumstance that persuaded me to set up my next camp here. Moreover, it was in line with the originally planned route.

[Border of Kiowa Territory
between the northern Arkansas
and Canadian rivers]

July 14. We were on our way very early and advanced eleven miles due west when we chanced on a beautiful brook bubbling with springs, which rushed through the lovely valley with a tremendous roar, like a silver ribbon among the green meadows. The shores of the brook are thickly lined with clusters of poplars, and a certain species of grape grows among them in fabulous abundance. It unquestionably belongs to the local flora. These grapevines are only four feet high and are as evenly spaced as if they were planted by someone. One of their main characteristics, which makes them differ from all other wild grapes, is that they are not climbers but stand erect like any other dwarf bush, and one can judge their abundance if I state that they cover about eight square miles. I stripped one bush out of curiosity and weighed it. It came to seven bushels.

Apparently this creek is the favorite wintering place of many Indian families, for we found many tent sites and for miles the shore is lined with poplar poles whose foliage was eaten by horses and mules. Almost every prairie Indian tribe feeds its favorite horses and mules with the bark of the poplar, so perhaps the abundance of young poplars is one of the things that draws them here. We also saw many stumps of poplars which were chopped down from year to year. Some were

6. *The Arkansas River, One-Half Mile from Its Source*, original drawing by Xántus, August 1, 1856; print by Rohn, Pest, 1858.

rotting with age while others were so fresh that the sap was still flowing. The fine mesquite and grama grasses, which are green all through the winter, provide good grazing, and when additional fodder is needed poplar branches easily fill the need.

At present we are on the border of Kiowa territory, which is between the northern Arkansas and Canadian rivers, and it is probable that most of the tribe winters here. I am convinced that it would be easy to meet them here in the winter, and this would also be desirable because so little is known about them.

Game is plentiful. Our hunters are able to provide the expedition with fresh meat daily, so much so that out of the twenty-five cattle we brought along I have not used one yet and hope there won't be any need to do so. Today, for example, we shot eleven deer and two antelope. We suffer greatly from the lack of greens; we have not eaten any for almost four months, except for some wild garlic. Already at Elk Creek more than once the symptoms of scurvy appeared among us and I have taken every possible precaution for the prevention of this fearsome disease. With the exception of a few dried apples and some lemon juice, I have no antiscurvy specific at my disposal, and so I grasp every opportunity to utilize the flora of the territory through which we travel. I bade my men to eat any halfway edible greens they can find. The grapes and plums, on the other hand, caused diarrhea, which scared me and nearly exhausted my medical knowledge. With the exception of a few cases, I cured them all with opium and lead acid, and right now there is no further sign of it in my party. Amidst all this, it was a pleasant discovery when we found a large tract of wild onions. I deployed the entire personnel and we collected about three tons and loaded it on the wagons. I believe it will benefit all of us during the long journey still ahead.

[Near the tri-state junction of Kansas, Oklahoma, and Colorado, between the north fork of the Cimarron and Arkansas Rivers.]

July 16. This evening we reached the last stream which feeds the southern fork of the Arkansas, and we are in the neighborhood of the last significant creek which empties into this fork from the north. Its source originates in a pleasant poplar grove only three miles from us. In this same grove, at the base of a tall poplar which stands isolated at water's edge, I buried a bottle with the following note in it: "On July 16, 1856, an exploring expedition camped here. It was under the command of John Xántus, assisted by William Hammond, assistant engineer, John Harling and John Burke, chief wagon masters, 22 hunters and carters."* There are crosses marked on the tree north and south, and on the eastern side I carved this inscription: "John Xántus's exploring expedition, July 16, 1856."

The same evening an event took place which caused great anxiety to the entire camp. Charles Harling left the camp without my knowledge, very likely to "botanize," which was his custom. We only noticed his absence at supper time, and since there were many Indian tracks all around us we were greatly worried that he would fall into Indian hands. I immediately dispatched the Delaware to search for him and gave orders to fire the mortars they were carrying with them at ten minute intervals, and at the same time made preparations to look for him myself with a few well-armed men. Before the second charge of the mortar was fired, however, Harling stepped into a tent, completely confused and bewildered in the manner of people who are lost. The summary of his long story was that at three in the afternoon he left the camp in search of insects and flowers. On his way back he lost sight of the camp as he crossed a hillock on the high prairie. Turning first right then left trying to find his direction he became so confused that at sunset, when he caught sight of the camp no more than a half-mile away, he thought it was Kiowa or southern Comanche camp. He hid in the tall grass, and it was getting dark when he heard the first mortar charge, which revived him, and he joyfully hurried back. We hardly slept all night from laughter which was fed again by the "doctor," as we called our friend Hammond, because he was always doctoring himself and carried a whole pharmacy with him.

July 17–19. On the seventeenth, with Harling, three Indians and five hunters, I rode off to the south in search of the Canadian River. Our direction took us at once into the high plateau of Llano Estacado, where the human eye cannot rest on a fixed point anywhere on the horizon; it was just like a lonely bark plunging every which way in the

*See Introduction.   107

great solitude of the southern seas. The limitless flat plain spreads in every direction—right, left, front, and back, wherever the eye can see. Never have I seen such dismal monotony.

After riding nearly fifteen miles on this seemingly endless plain, our eyes all at once beheld a rock cliff beyond which spread a valley. I instantly recognized it as the environs of the Canadian River and I was not mistaken, for after ten miles of further travel we stopped at the bank of the river. A straight line of twenty-five miles from the headwaters of the southern Arkansas brought us to these shores. This gave me immense satisfaction, for it proved the accuracy of my geographical calculations as to the origin of the southern Arkansas.

Around noon, when the vertical rays of the sun heat the earth and the layers of air closest to it, we usually experience a shimmering movement of the air on the Llano Estacado, which sometimes conjures up imaginary and illusive mirages on the horizon. This phenomenon, for which the French army in Africa paid a heavy price, and which is also experienced in the Bánát and Temes regions of the Hungarian plain, is nowhere in the world as magnificent as on the Llano Estacado. The extraordinary refraction of the air produced distant objects in fantastic and wildly distorted forms and often in such enormously enlarged sizes and shapes that the effect is truly astounding. For example, a buzzard or crow appears as large as a tall Slovak grenadier in his bearskin tchako.* More than once we mistook an antelope or rabbit for a horse or buffalo. When one travels on these thirsty plains, the appearance around noon time of beautiful lakes and rivers surrounded by green groves and lawns is most refreshing. The heart beats faster in the hope that within a very short time one will sip the cooling and invigorating water. One digs one's spurs into the shank of the tired horse and urges and urges and wonders why he has not yet reached his Eden. At last, dispirited, he realizes that the promised land was in the realm of a fata morgana. Later it appears again, as if he were nearer his objective. Once again it seems real and he rushes forward with revived spirits but is forced to realize that the mirage is further and further away and is unattainable. Thus, he advances mile after mile, never reaching his goal, when suddenly there is a change in the air which blurs the objects already seen and produces others in another direction, until the thirsty wanderer is convinced that it is only the fata morgana playing games.

---

*Slovak grenadiers wore the kind of bearskin tchako associated with the Coldstream Guards.

This evening the northwesterly wind brought fairly heavy rain, which encouraged us to hope that we would find sufficient water everywhere. From the tabulation of my meteorological observations it is clear that our barometer was a dependable forecaster during our entire journey. Very often two to three days before a rain there was such an unusual drop in the mercury that it surprised all of us. It never did start to rain, however, until the barometer returned to its normal grade. After questioning many Indians, I concluded that from the middle of May to the middle of August there is hardly any rain at this latitude and longitude and seldom even dew during this season beyond the ninety-ninth degree of longitude. The contents of creeks and rivers are mostly absorbed in the fissures and crevices of the beds. Water is scarcely visible and the vegetation suffers greatly from the aridity.

In total contrast to the generally proclaimed weather, we were so fortunate that nature made an exception for us by blessing us with plentiful rains. Often our clothes were still wet from the dew from eight to nine in the morning as we were riding in tall weeds. The streams, rivers and lakes provided us with abundant water, and the prairie seemed to be smiling with all its lush, emerald countenance. Near the place where we pitched camp today, we found an old Indian camp, which was the site of a battle two months ago, according to our Delaware interpreter. He deduced this from the remnants of a large pyre which we discovered, where the fallen bodies, tents and tools of the enemy were sacrificed in the flames to the war god. Tent poles, partially melted glass beads, iron hoops, and other household and war tools were scattered around the fire and seemed to have escaped from the all-consuming flames. Judging by the tent sites, the defeated party was not large in number.

Also today we came upon the tracks of a Kiowa band which moved from southeast to north before the last rain. Hardly a day passes that we do not find signs of their presence, and it is surprising that we have not yet met them. They are probably hunting buffalo in the valleys of the Kow and Smoky rivers, and only when these animals move southward will they move on to the valleys of the Arkansas, Canadian and Red Rivers, where during the winter they will find an adequate supply of mesquite and grama grass to feed their horses and mules.

Until now we have been gradually ascending to a higher altitude in our westerly direction, and the present state of the barometer indicates that we are 2,702 feet above sea level.

On our way today alongside the river valley we ran into a great many prairie dogs. I tried to get a few to have them stuffed, and so I shot a good many of the largest ones, but the charge from the drawn barrel rifle damaged them so much that I did not think it worthwhile to have even one stuffed, and decided that I will use my other rifle in the future.

[Somewhere in southeast Colorado]

July 26. All day today our track led through a seemingly endless "dog city." (The scientific name of this interesting animal, [the prairie dog] which in many respects resembles the Hungarian hamster, is *Spermo philus ludoviceanus.*) The whole area was crowded with their lairs, so that many times we had to change our course in order to avoid the great piles of dirt heaped in front of their holes. Whoever traverses this "dog city" can see large numbers of these little creatures in every direction sitting in front of their holes. Their earsplitting screams and constant barking numb the senses. It would not take too much imagination for the traveler to think that he is near a large and noisy city.

The unbelievable multitude of these little animals becomes most apparent when one looks over the large area which their villages occupy, and in the true sense of the word, completely cover.

For example, the city through which we passed today is every bit of twenty-five miles in length; its width I could not determine, for neither to the right nor left were the limits discernable. Assuming a minimum width of twenty-five miles, the extent of the entire city would be 625 English square miles. Considering that their holes are about twenty yards apart (in every hole there are about five dogs), if one would care to calculate the population, he would quickly be convinced that this is the most densely populated city in the world.

This very interesting species of mammal is found all over the western prairies from Mexico to Canada. Travelers who have wandered over one part or another of the prairies have often mentioned them. Still, I have discovered certain facts about their customs and mode of life which have not been noted elsewhere, as far as I know. I will attempt to further somewhat our knowledge of their life style. They greatly enjoy family life. The locations of the villages are always chosen with the food supply in mind, which consists of a short, smooth, silky weed found only on the high prairie and often fifty to 100 miles from any visible source of water. For example, I saw a village in the southern region of the Canadian River that was about forty miles from the nearest water, and, in fact, I doubt if there was water even at a depth of 100 feet. I do believe that these animals are able to exist without water for very long periods, which is an important fact, for all other mammals would perish within a much shorter time from the lack of this vital element.

Moreover, there is no rain or dew all through the summer on these prairies, and, as the dogs never venture far from their lair, I can state positively that they do not consume any water, beyond the little that their food, the grass, contains. It is also a fact that they hibernate underground during the winter and spend the cold months in lethargic sleep. They don't gather food for the winter. By October the grass has dried up around their holes, and at times the ground freezes stone hard, which makes it impossible for them to get food in a normal manner.

When the animal senses that the time for hibernation is nearing (usually by the end of October), he seals his sleeping quarters all around to shut out the cold air, and arranges everything to ensure a safe and comfortable winter sleep. Finally, when the time comes, he seals up the entrance as well. He stays in this position until the first warm days of spring, when he opens his door and sits cheerfully in front of his house, as he did last year and the year before.

I have heard from many Indians that in the autumn, just before the first cold storm, all the inhabitants of the "dog city" can be seen, busy as bees, gathering twigs, thick weeds, and dirt, and sealing the entrances in spite of the biting cold, although this is usually followed by nice warm weather. This is the Indian's infallible barometer.

This proves that instinct teaches these quadrupeds when to expect good or bad weather and to adjust their activities accordingly. It is worth mentioning the curious fact that a species of small owl is their inseparable cohabitant. One can see these owls in numbers almost as large, sitting in front of the entrances when the dogs are away, and on top of the mounds when the dog family is in its chambers. Why this friendship between owl and dog? I have never been able to discover the reason, although I have examined every possible basis of common interest. It must be left, therefore, to a more knowledgeable and cleverer natural scientist than I. My only advice would be to consider whether it is possible that they find food among the dogs. They do not live, however, in the same hole as the dog; on the contrary, when 111 people approach them they always fly away instead of hiding in the hole.

I have read in Captain Wilkes' *Travels* that every dog hole is also inhabited by a rattlesnake.* This is a mere fable, however, and is similar to the Don Quixote type of fable of my compatriot Haraszthy, for I wandered days on end through such dog colonies and saw 100 to 400 scattered dog houses more than once without ever finding a single rattlesnake. Undoubtedly one can find a rattler once in a while in a dog hole; I did so myself. That is why some people have claimed that they are the house guests of the dogs and live together. But I am thoroughly convinced that such arrangement would be contrary to the best interests of the dog family, for the rattlers eat the young dogs. This conviction was confirmed the other day when I killed a huge rattlesnake and found in its stomach a not-quite-digested but fully grown prairie dog.

Xántus also takes issue with Stansbury, who said of the prairie dogs:

> They are very hard to get, as they are never found far from their holes, and when shot, fall immediately into them, where they are generally guarded by a rattlesnake—the usual sharer of their subterranean retreat. Several were shot by us in this situation, but when the hand was about to be thrust into the hole to draw them out, the ominous rattle of this dreaded reptile would be instantly heard, warning the intruder of the danger he was about to incur. A little white borrowing owl (Stryx cuniculiara) also is frequently found taking up his abode in the same domicile. (Captain Howard Stansbury, An Expedition to the Valley of the Great Salt Lake of Utah [London: Samson Low, Son & Co., p. 37, originally published by order of the U.S. Senate by Lippincott, Grambo & Co., Philadelphia, 1852].)

July 27. Today again we traveled over dog colonies, and it is very likely that because of their great number the Indians named this main southern branch of the river *Ke-che-a-qui-ho-ho* or "Prairie Dog City River."

Today I suffered an almost irreplaceable loss. I lost my best "bear catcher" dog. He was a gift from Senator Gibson of Leavenworth. He

---

*Charles Wilkes, *Western America, Including California and Oregon* (Philadelphia, Lea & Blanchard, 1849).

took a great deal of trouble and effort to get me this valiant animal. I regret this all the more as we shall soon reach a region* where we shall no doubt encounter many bears, and we shall sorely miss the sharp teeth of our friend Rollo.

Toward evening we reconnoitered the area and about eight miles from our camp, in a deep ravine, we came upon a band of Kiowa Indians. At first they were greatly confused and ran in all directions; later, however, our Delaware scout managed to have a word with one of them and explained our friendly intentions. Soon after that they all came around and we had an amiable pow-wow. Their chief told us that they were on their annual pilgrimage to the graveside of their leader, fallen in a famous battle ten years ago. Our Delaware interpreter related with so much feeling the heroic deeds of the fallen hero and painted his life in such romantic colors that I begged the chief to show me the grave. He willingly acceded, jumped on his horse and offered to guide me. Not more than three miles to the southeast we came to a deep valley where we could only descend by dismounting and leading our horses, rather than jumping them over the boulders on the mountainside. When we reached the bottom of the valley, I was surprised at the beauty of the landscape around us. The entire valley was covered with dense *eczetta* and hackberry bushes, interspersed with tall cedar and pine trees. At last, after a half-hour trek through shoulder-high grass, our guide stopped at a dark and dense spot, took off his headfeathers and pointed mutely to Xonk Mely's grave a few yards from us.

By the time I dismounted and approached it there were many Indians squatting on the heavy and artificially decorated columns of the grave. Their expression and whole attitude spoke unmistakably of such great grief and loss that it was contagious. In the deathly silence I took off my hat and spoke a few words appropriate to the place and occasion, while all of us knelt down spontaneously and prayed for the peace of the dead and the welfare of his nation. It was obvious that the Indians understood, if not the words the intent of our action, for they embraced us, shook our hands and kept repeating in a sing-song *Sosam kuja, sosam kuja kevet.* (You are good friends, good friends, thank you.)

July 29. Realizing that we cannot continue with our wagons alongside this river, I have decided to leave my caravan behind under the command of my friend Hammond, and with one Indian, in the

*Near the border of Kansas and Colorado in the foothills of the Rocky Mountains.

company of Harling and ten well armed men, I will push forward and follow the river all the way to its source.

We packed provisions for ten days on four mules and left this morning in a cheerful mood to traverse very rough terrain. We discovered in a ravine a gypsum cave of rare beauty, which was apparently formed by water erosion; its entrance resembled a beautifully sculptured triumphal arch, while the inside walls were smooth as polished marble, showing three distinctive layers. The topmost was green, the center one orange, and the bottom one white. These colors blended in such well-ordered proportions that they surpassed the beauty of even the most exquisite rainbow. Having reached this point, we were exhausted from the effort of trekking over the mountains and valleys; also we were extremely thirsty. Fortunately, very near the cave we found an ice-cold spring bubbling through the granite wall, and although it tasted of lime, we had our fill almost to the bursting point and felt none the worse for it.

It was almost impossible to continue to the top of the ridge, since the tongues of men and beast were hanging out from weariness; after a short rest at the cave, we descended the gorge to the river. Unfortunately, the water was as bitter as gall, undrinkable, so we preferred not to quench our thirst. On top of all this was the extreme heat. At two in the afternoon the thermometer showed 114° in the shade. There was not the slightest movement of air, and wherever we looked there was nothing but chalk and gypsum, reflecting the rays of the sun, causing our eyes and heads to ache.

In spite of all these unpleasant difficulties, we continued until sunset, when at last we settled down for the night next to a murky water hole.

At sunrise at last we reached a point where the river split into two almost equal-sized branches. Without hesitation we took the left branch, because it seemed a little wider, and soon we left behind the rock walls, as they receded from the shores, forming a level plain between the cliffs and the river. This was a tremendous contrast to the formidable cliffs. The plain was covered with rich green grass, with here and there lush raspberries. We also saw some hickory and ash trees. This pleasing sight cheered us no end, and although our thirst was never greater, our spirits had lifted.*

---

*It is difficult to pinpoint the exact area but the terrain suggests it might be the Royal Gorge, west of Pueblo, Colorado, just south of Pike's Peak.

Physically we had reached a point of extreme lassitude, having trudged over the eternal uniformity of jagged peaks, barren cliffs and deep, bottomless, desolate gorges. After another twenty-eight miles we pitched camp on the shore of the main branch, where the river is only eighty yards wide and rushes over its sandy bed on to the northeast with a great roar.

We suffered much from the river water which made us nauseous, yet necessity forced us to live with it. Many among us were racked with cruel cramps and vomiting, but I must admit no one complained and the efforts to make light of and joke about this predicament were most praiseworthy. The main and exclusive topic of conversation was the various refreshing drinks and ice cream available in great abundance and for a pittance in every small town or village. My companions tried to figure out how much money they would make if they had a large store of iced lemonade on hand. As a variation, everyone announced how much they would be willing to pay for a glass of iced water or a dish of ice cream, were they available. For example, one mule driver swore that for a milk pail full of good iced water he would gladly exchange all his tangible and intangible fortune of $1,000. Of course all the offers were made with the full realization of their unreality; no one expected to be offered ice cream or lemonade for hard cash.

July 31. We saddled up early this morning. The river narrowed into a channel hardly twenty yards wide and the bottom, which is sandy all the way to the junction with the Mississippi, suddenly changed into rocks and boulders. The water roaring over them became crystal clear instead of the murky reddish color we had found until now, and to our indescribable joy it was free of salt. Whoever has followed our tribulations can well imagine how this unexpected good fortune heartened and raised our spirits.

We certainly made up for all our suffering by drinking without stop by the pailful while following the twisting course of the river in the narrow mountain pass, until we came to a point where the river was completely blocked by huge granite and porphyry boulders, reminding one if not of the Last Judgment, at least of the Fall of Jericho, as described so explicitly in the Bible. We just stood there spellbound, gaping at this chaotic clutter of nature, this magnificent jumble.

Our horses and mules secured and left behind, we put on deerskin moccasins and, with the help of hooks and crampons, pushed forward and up the steep rocks to find our ultimate destination. 115

The gigantic sandstone cliffs, more than 1,000 feet high, became narrower with each step, until they formed a circle of no more than a few yards, and joined overhead, creating a narrow but long corridor at the end of which is the source of the main branch of the Arkansas River. The spring bursts forth from the bottom of the rock cave and, rushing over the piles of huge boulders, begins its long course, with its countless small tributaries, until it reaches its final destination, the Mississippi, helping to make it one of the mightiest rivers in the world.

In the immediate vicinity of the source we found two small poplars, on which we carved the date and purpose of our presence.

As we view this small stream and its twisting course, rumbling down the gorge of the mountain pass, we find it hard to realize that this small waterway will grow into one of the greatest and most important rivers of America, over which more than 800 steamboats cruise a distance of 2,000 miles, and which irrigates the largest and richest valley of the known world.

We gorged our yearning stomachs with the ice-cold spring water. The wild beauty and the majestic magnitude of the mountains amply compensated us for our trials and ordeals. As we neared the source, the grandeur of the scene surpassed anything I have seen in my life, perhaps even Niagara. I must admit my inability to describe adequately the feeling of joy that filled my entire being upon gazing at nature's masterpiece.

The steely grip of endless time and the relentless erosion of water chiseled and sculpted such fantastic shapes that it takes no great imagination to see them as great works of art forming a grandiose vista. One is filled with humility in contemplation of the greatness of Creation and the realization of how puny and fleeting is human existence and competence in contrast to nature's eternity.

With the help of hooks and improvised rope ladders we climbed to the top of the ridge above the source and found ourselves on the plateau of Llano Estacado, which from here to the Rio Grande mountain range, forms an uninterrupted desert.

The geographical location of this point is 37° 15′ northern latitude and 106° 7′ 11″ western longitude, and based on my barometric observations, I estimated the altitude at the source as being 3,450 feet above sea level.

Yesterday and the day before we saw many bear tracks and sometimes the animals themselves, but not having good dogs, we shot only two of them.

Our Delaware Indian, who rides one of our wildest and most untamable horses, wanted to do battle with a bear today, but because of the stubbornness of the horse, he could not get closer to it than ten paces. It is true, few horses dare to approach a bear. According to our scouts the American black bear (*Ursus americanus pall*) is much smarter than many other quadrupeds. For example, when it is ready to lie down for a rest, it goes a few hundred feet in the direction of the wind, leaving behind its tracks; thus, a possible pursuer following the tracks would also have to go in the direction of the wind, and the bear's keen sense of smell would immediately enable it to detect the scent of impending danger and depart in time. When pursued, it often hides in underground caves, from which hunters usually try to smoke it out by setting a fire at the opening of the cave. It has happened more than once, however, that when the smoke becomes too irritating the bear determinedly rushes at the fire, trying to scatter it with its paws. Still, it does not leave its cave, but returns to its depths. These and other tales prove that the bear knows the relationship between cause and effect but, according to other stories, it was considered one of the stupidest of creatures. I was told that often when the smoke and fire would not drive the bear out the hunter would go right after it into the cave with a torch. One would think this a most daring act and that the bear without any further ado would turn on its uninvited guest. But instead, as soon as it saw the approaching light, it would squat on its hind legs, cover its eyes and face with its paws and just sit still until the light was removed. In this way, without exposing himself to any danger, the hunter could approach the bear at will, take aim, and crush his skull. Four different Indians attested to the validity of this claim, and I have no reason to doubt them, as they are experienced hunters.

The black bear is normally harmless unless it is wounded or its cubs are nearby. When protecting its cubs, its savagery and desperate struggles are unsurpassed. Under such circumstances, it would often attack a man on horseback and chase him for miles.

August 3. This evening we returned from the source of the river to our camp, following the same route that we took when we came here, and found everyone in good health and the camp in good order. Our friends were waiting for our return with much anxiety.

August 7. One of our Delaware Indians shot a big wild cat (*Lyncus rufus cav*) today, which I stuffed, as is my custom. At the same time I loaded our collection of naturalia on the wagons, which were emptied by 117 our diminishing provisions. Altogether there are already more than 300 snakes, 200 lizards, 700 fish, turtles, and so on, forty-six reams of plants and nearly 1,500 hundredweight of minerals, many birds, mammals, insects, many flasks of water (for chemical analysis), and so on, collected for the Smithsonian Institution.* After my arrival I forwarded the entire collection to its destination and received this response:

"Smithsonian Institution, Washington, October 6, 1856. Sir: The 26 cases of naturalia which you, as the head of the expedition exploring the Arkansas River collected with such praiseworthy diligence, carrying out the order of the President, arrived. The departments are already cataloguing and describing the collection soon to be published and it will be my pleasant duty to inform you when this occurs. Until then accept our sincere thanks. Your obedient servant, etc. B. Girard"

August 15. Today I shot a fat stag and our hunters bagged three more deer, so we have enough fresh meat. All in all, our excellent hunters have amply provided us with the needed meat so far on this journey, so we did not have to touch the cattle originally intended for slaughter. Our Indians use their magic whistles even to hunt deer, which greatly amuses us, for the sound produced a panther and two wolves. The Delaware particularly favor hunting with this whistle, and usually they meet with great success. The whistle resembles the mouthpiece of a clarinet. It is really a narrow, thin brass tube. With a little practice, one can use it to imitate exactly the bleat of a fawn. They usually use the whistle in June and July, when the fawns are still with their mothers. The hunter takes a position on the edge of a grove where he suspects hinds may be present. The hind usually stays with the fawn only for nursing, after which she retires into a brush and lies down. But when she hears the whining sound of the whistle, which carries about half a mile, she rushes wildly to the aid of the whining fawn she believes to be in danger, but instead meets a death-dealing

---

*It is recorded in the annual report of the Smithsonian Institution for 1857 that Dr. Hammond, surgeon in Lieutenant Bryan's exploring party at Bridger's Pass, made an interesting collection and that he was assisted in this for a time by Mr. J. Xántus de Vesey (p. 47). In the same report, J. X. de Vesey and Dr. W. A. Hammond (in that order) were acknowledged as the donors of birds and mammals from Kansas (p. 54). Similar recognition was given in the reports of the Pacific Railroad Surveys, vols. 8 and 9. "These gifts were important in advancing Xántus's career, for Professor Baird delighted in rewarding with the support of his official position those who enriched the collections of the Smithsonian Institution." H. M. Madden, *Xántus, Hungarian Naturalist in the Pioneer West*, p. 44.

bullet. I do not consider this kind of hunt chivalrous, and if it were up to me I would permit it only in case of extreme need for food.

Often, upon hearing the sound of this whistle, not only do panthers or wolves appear, but bears as well, in the expectation of finding the flesh of a fawn. You would think that this noble species would soon be on the verge of extinction, as it is pursued not only by hunters but by so many huge beasts of prey. But there is no cause for concern. Providence offers special protection to the weak and young fawn. It is well known that older deer leave a strong scent which is sooner or later detected by pursuing hounds, who are thus able to trap the lagging deer. But the young fawn has no scent at all, and neither dog nor beast will pursue her unless she is seen. The fact that they are not exterminated while young by so many beasts is due to this wise protection.

For the past few days we have been suffering from the annoyance of huge black horseflies, which attacked our livestock with remarkable impudence. No sooner do they alight on one than they leave punctures dripping with blood. These and another small green wine fly were the only irritating insects we encountered throughout our trip.

Two of our wagoneers who were suffering from scurvy during the entire trip are still not well, and I greatly fear that unless we soon find some wild onions they will meet a fatal end. I always try to have the entire staff constantly use all the anti-scurvy medicines included in our food supply, as well as the wild plants we gathered. But all these are insufficient to prevent or cure the disease once it is contracted, when for an extended period of time one lives exclusively on venison or under conditions which predispose susceptibility to the disease. Furthermore, the personnel is not too keen about using the drugs supplied by the commissary, because the fixed costs are deducted from their pay or from their staples (zwieback, tea, sugar, coffee, beans, rice, salt, and so on), which at best are none too ample for people who are on their feet day and night, engaged in very fatiguing work. The special food which my friend Hammond and I had bought for our own personal use, we have put at the disposal of the scurvy sufferers—so much so that we ourselves are beginning to feel the lack of it. Still, our humane act was to no avail, and so I have come to believe that there is little one can do if there is a complete lack of greens in the diet. We found a lot of grapes today in the mountains, which we hope will be of benefit to our ailing comrades.

August 17. The particular territory which embraces the Wichita mountain range belonged for many years to the Wichita Indians. By tradition, they have absolute and valid rights. According to their belief, they were born in these mountain ranges; the "great spirit" bestowed the entire territory to them and their descendants and they have occupied it ever since. However, in spite of these claims, which are based on the legal principle of first occupancy and actual possession, the entire territory down to the 100th western longitude was presented by Congress to the Choctaw Indians, provided they would move here from northern Texas, where they presently live. It is not easy to understand by what right this was done. The Wichita are insignificant numerically, consisting of no more than 5,000 families all told; thus, they are not well-equipped to press their claims and to defend them by force, if necessary. Yet the American government is not likely to reconsider their claims—all the more so as they are the most inveterate and brazen horse thieves. Northern Texan and New Mexican settlers could testify to this, to their sorrow. In fact, a few years ago they invaded the state of Missouri with unheard of audacity, driving off more than 500 horses and mules and shooting down with arrows all those who resisted. No one has penetrated their mountains within living memory. Like the Chinese, they are extremely jealous of their land and most reluctant to open it to strangers. They have chased from their borders not only private expeditions but also the military, dispatched by the government.

At present we are camped on the shore of a swift creek with clear water, and near us there are several cold springs; only now can we tell the difference between good and bad water, after being too well acquainted with the latter in the unforgettable environs of the Prairie Dog River. Following the creek upward about three miles from our camp, I found its source on the side of the valley, as it burst forth from a granite crevice.

Next to us, or rather below us, the valley spreads, surrounded on three sides by steep, sharp-peaked mountains, covered almost in their entirety with a dense forest. Trees of all kinds are in great abundance. The oaks are mostly straight, thick and tall, and eminently suitable for sawmills. The soil is exceptionally fertile; it nearly sinks under the weight of the rich vegetation.

August 18. Our direction today is once again to the north. Proceeding upward in the valley of the creek we came upon a breach in the upper range of the mountain chain, through which we managed, with superhuman effort, to pull our wagons. The breach, while not situated too high, was criss-crossed with deep fissures, which were barricaded in many places by huge granite boulders; at other places it sloped so sharply that we all had to support each wagon with our arms, inching ahead one at a time lest they fall into the depths below.

We had to use all our physical strength to get through the pass. Finally, our last wagon was moved onto the north side, and after a few miles of further progress we found ourselves on the shores of a good-sized river, where we promptly set up camp. This is at the foot of the highest peak of the Wichita Mountains. This terrifying and unscaleable peak, the highest in the entire mountain chain (7,400 feet), I named Mount Cooper in memory of the beloved poet who gained so many faithful and warm friends with his romances about the poor Indian tribes.

This jagged peak, which overshadows all the others in the background, gives a majestic aspect to an otherwise forbidding landscape. It also serves for many miles as a guidepost, not only for travelers but also for Indian hunters. Our altitude at this point, according to the barometer and triangulation by sextant, is 1,945 feet above sea level.

The valley spreading north of Mount Cooper is one of the most beautiful I have ever seen. It is approximately five miles wide, edged with two fantastically shaped mountain chains, in the center of which a charming little creek flows its twisting course. It is fifty yards wide and three to four feet deep; its water is crystal clear. It plunges wildly and endlessly with a crashing sound from one fall to another with great zest. The creek is full of beaver, and it is teeming with trout to such an extent that one would think there is not enough room for them in the water. Both banks of the creek are covered with tall and slender pecan palms; here and there are water oak, white ash, maple, and beech trees and blackberry bushes. Higher upon the foothills, white oaks are plentiful and on the slopes red cedars flutter in the breeze.

The valley is exceptionally fertile, rich vegetation covering it everywhere. The grass is dense and of good quality and is five to seven feet high; if the big flies were not attacking them so ferociously, our livestock would have a veritable feast.

Near our camp we came upon another caprice of nature. Two huge, solitary red granite boulders rose from the prairie to a height of 300 feet with a diameter of 275 feet.

Toward evening I shouldered my rifle and rode off to go deer hunting on my Negro servant's pony. Hardly a mile from the camp, I noticed a peacefully grazing buffalo bull on the bank of the creek among some oak trees. As soon as I caught sight of him he raised his shaggy mane, looked at me and took off. I too immediately spurred on my pony, urging the poor little beast to run as fast as it could, cutting across the prairie so as to catch the bull on the side, if not the front. Exhausting the pony's capacity, the closest I could get to the bull was 200 paces, and so, with a parting shot of "good health to you" I let him go—not without annoyance—and ambled back home.

August 19. At sunup we crossed the creek, after hacking space on both banks to maneuver our wagons up and then down. We traveled downward in the valley following the edge of the forest onto the prairie. The countryside is identical to that through which we passed yesterday, just as beautiful and fertile. Around noon we entered two abandoned Indian villages. Our Delaware claimed that they were inhabited by Wichita and Keechee. The frames of many wigwams were still standing. Extensive maize and tobacco fields were visible here and there, covered with ten-to-twelve-foot-high weeds.

Our camp on the bank of the creek is about two miles above the village, where the Wichita allegedly lived before they moved further into the mountains. It would seem they lived here for many years, diligently and extensively cultivating maize, tobacco, cucumber, melon, and different kinds of squash and bean. Everything indicates that they exercised great consideration and care when they chose this place to settle. It is located under the easternmost slope of the mountains on a high plateau on the southern bank of the creek, rising about 200 feet above the water level, with a picturesque view of the entire area toward the northeast and south. The high location was carefully chosen for protection against sudden attack, and the natural advantages are ideal for defense.

The landscape now unfolds before the eye the beauty of nature in its every imaginable variety. Mountains and hills, peaks and woods, groves and lakes, waterfalls and meadows, look as if they were in a natural park. One is irresistibly drawn to it. We are leaving it with regret, much like bidding good-bye to an old friend whom we shall, in all probability, never see again.

Undoubtedly, this was a favorite habitat of the Wichita and I cannot understand why they left it, unless it was for fear of the Comanche. According to our Delaware Indian, it was only two years ago that they abandoned their village, which assertion is borne out by the perfect condition of the wigwam poles and corn driers.

The fertility of the land truly surpasses everything we have seen on our trip. On what used to be maize and tobacco fields the vegetation is so dense that it is impossible to advance even a few steps on horseback. Furthermore, even our dogs are unable to get through. At places the weeds are almost twenty feet high, criss-crossed with ivy of all varieties, so that we had to use our axes to hack our way to pick some of the flowers. It is easy to surmise what this land would produce with only a minimum of care. There are so many forests, so that the farmer would have an ample supply of building material and firewood.

Practically all the species of the North American hardwoods are found here in exceptionally good quality. The highly valued and incomparable Spanish oak for shingles is quite common here (*Quercus elongata*). On the meadows we saw gorgeous so-called "Flaming Love," or "Passion Flower," in countless varieties (*Passiflora incarnata*), and we have added two hitherto unknown specimen of "touch-me-nots" (*noli me tangere*) to our plant collection.

In the afternoon our company returned from the exploration of the mountains and, to my astonishment, brought news that we have stumbled upon an enormous coalfield. I rode off at once, hurrying to the scene to personally inspect the find. Great was my amazement, not only to be able to verify the news, but to find the entire mountain range covered with coal. The upper stratum is quite coarse and not of usable quality, but digging to a depth of fifteen feet we came upon the richest layer of the finest quality anthracite. We collected several samples at different depths, which I sent to the Patent Office upon my return.* They sent them to the chemical laboratory of Armstead University, and upon examination they were found to be the purest and finest quality coal.

Having reached at last the eastern branch of the Wichita Mountains, tomorrow morning we shall cross the creek and turn our wagons homeward—that is, set our compass needle for the shortest route to Elk Creek.

I must not fail to say what I feel so deeply—that the more time we spent in this region and the better we got to know it, the more pleasure we derived from it and the harder it was to depart. All my life

---

*There is no record of this in the Patent Office.

an irresistible longing drew me to the land, and I must confess that I have seen few places in my life that offer comparable advantages for successful farming as does this. Needless to say, within a few years this area will be subjected to intensive industrialization. The rich forests, beautiful meadows, the immense quantity of granite, gypsum and coal, but especially the fertile soil, will soon attract the economic forces. Once the axe of the pioneer breaks the deep silence of the forest, it will quickly be followed by the pickaxe and hammer of the miner in the mountains. The sawmill and the forge will compete in the building of railroads, which will haul the surplus produce and magically transform it into solid gold. If an enterprising company, even with limited capital with which to purchase the needed equipment, should locate here within the next few years, I would state with mathematical certainty that within a decade it would reach such a degree of affluence that it would be the envy of the richest nabob. The choicest forests could be taken possession of now, as well as the most advantageous locations. The cultivation of the land could be expended from year to year and cattle, sheep, and horses could be raised in great numbers. By the time civilization reached here, the company would be so well established and in so dominant a position that it could sell its surplus products to the newcomers at high prices. It would take years for newcomers to attain the same degree of development. Nature endowed this land with such generosity that it seems to be saying, "Here you must settle."

Only one circumstance would offer any difficulty, but it would be by no means insurmountable. The best lands are those on the latitude and longitude Congress has bestowed to the Choctaw Indians, as I previously mentioned. However, the Wichita region is as yet far from being civilized or settled, and being near the Comanche, the Choctaw have not taken advantage of their title to the land and, in fact, may not even know about it, having never come up from the prairies. The owners of countless millions of acres of fertile land at the northern border of Texas, and at the sources of the Red River, they are perfectly content and prefer their peaceful existence closer to civilization. They have shed all their ancient customs and given up their dependence on the uncertainty of hunting. They live in orderly villages, and are occupied with agriculture, cattle raising, and commerce. Their attitude toward the savage Indians is the same as that of the white man. They have many schools, their own Choctaw literature, and seven newspapers printed in their own language. In short, one can hardly recognize them as Indians.

If some company should want to settle in the Wichita Mountains, to insure itself against the uncertainties of the future (which I must confess are based on fantasy), it could easily and cheaply buy all the land it would want from the Choctaw and thus have a clear title.

August 20. We did not leave as early this morning as usual because we have lost one of our mules. At dawn two of our Delaware started to search for it but they came back having found no trace of it. So far we have been fortunate in not losing a single one of our livestock, so I was determined to do everything possible to find it. I spoke of my firm determination to John, our old interpreter, who did not participate in the first search, and asked him at the same time what he thought were the chances of success. He answered laconically, "Maybe yes, maybe no." Smilingly, I sent him off with the instruction not to abandon the search until there was not the slightest possibility of finding the mule. Then we packed up and started homeward in a straight line. We crossed the creek just below the abandoned Wichita village where it was flowing rapidly over its gravelly bed. On the eastern bank we traveled over a wide, watery field, covered with lush, ripening wild rice (*Oriza occidentalia*). Having struggled through the lowland, we emerged from the valley and continued in an easterly direction along the mountain range.

Our tireless and excellent hunter, John, showed up tonight at the camp with the lost mule. He tracked its traces for fifteen miles. He even shot a buffalo and brought back some of its meat. According to him the mule, after escaping from our camp, followed a twisting northerly trail left by the searching party. It was grazing but still continuing on its way when our friend John caught up with it. I asked him to tell me frankly if he had lost his patience during the long search. He answered categorically, "No," adding that since I gave him an order not to return without the mule, he would still be tracking it had he not been fortunate enough to find it so quickly. I have no doubt that our friend John would have acted according to his word, for I have met few men in my life who disregard pain, fatigue, and hardship to the extent that he does. Moreover, he has an exceptional sense of direction, and his judgment is always well-considered. All these traits, added to his extensive experience and familiarity with the grand prairies, eminently qualify him as a first-rate scout and caravan leader. He never passes the 125 most insignificant point without remembering it, in case fate should take him there again, even from an entirely different direction. When he finds himself in a locality, even if it is the first time in his life, after a brief inspection he will indicate the spot (if there is one) where water may be found, often in places where I could not see any indication of the presence of this essential element. This kind of service makes him an indispensable leader for an expedition like ours.

One story about John, told me by his Delaware companions, is particularly characteristic of him. Some years ago, on an assignment in the vicinity of the Red River, Captain Gunnison sent him to follow a footpath which apparently led into the mountains, and ordered him to report back the direction it took. John returned shortly and reported that the path did lead into the mountains but, in his opinion, not to any specific location. This being inadequate intelligence, the captain sent him out again with instructions to reconnoiter the footpath again and not to return without definite information. John set out a second time and did not return that day nor the following days. The mission traveled on, but John did not turn up. Day followed day without word from him, and it was believed certain that he had fallen into the hands of some roving Indians and had been slaughtered by them. Weeks after, when the mission arrived at last at the furthest settlements of the state of Arkansas, great was Gunnison's astonishment when he noticed John among those greeting him. John approached him with: "Captain, the footpath which you ordered me to follow ends right here." John had accomplished something that few others have ever done before and most probably even fewer will do in the future. He traversed hundreds of miles of barren prairie searching for the end of the footpath all by himself. His only means of support was his rifle. In spite of all this, he faithfully carried out his mission.

August 22. It rained all night. The soil was so soaked that we had difficulty pulling the wagons through. In spite of this we managed to progress about four miles over the swampy plain when I thought it best to set up camp. We had hardly pitched our tents when, in the woods on the other shore of the creek, a large band of Indians appeared. They had been unable to cross the rain-swollen creek. They asked us to span the creek with a few trees so that they might cross and "have a few words with the white captain." We complied and they came over on the poplar planks, floating their horses and mules, and set up camp near us.

7. *Kana Hexaya*, original drawing by Xántus, August 22, 1856; print by Rohn, Pest, 1858.

It was a Wichita hunting party numbering 156, under the leadership of Chief Kana Hexaya. They had a large number of horses and mules, most of them were overloaded with smoked venison and buffalo meat, the result of their hunt. Besides these, they had fifteen wild horses, which they had lassoed on the southern prairies. Their chiefs came to me and, after many embraces and handshakes, passed the peace pipe around. After these ceremonies, which are the indispensable prerequisites of Indian diplomacy, the head chief disclosed to us that upon hearing of our presence in their country, he had rushed here from a great distance to learn the purpose of our mission. In my answer, which John interpreted point by point, I stated with great gravity that we had been to the headwaters of the Arkansas River. I had visited the Indian nations there, as well as others on our way, to make friends with them and to extend to them the good wishes of the Great White Chief (as the Indians call the president), who had also instructed me to distribute a few gifts, as tokens of his good will, among those of his red sons who are the sincere friends of the white man. I further informed them that they would be held responsible for any future destruction or theft in the white settlements; therefore, they should not dare to harass or attack any traveling party going to California, otherwise they would have to contend with the anger of the Great White Chief and risk destruction by fire and sword. They agreed to everything and gave me their promise.

Then, upon inquiring about the headwaters of the Arkansas, they followed with interest the sketch I drew in the sand depicting the location of the lands traveled by our expedition. It seemed they were not acquainted with that distant region.

Toward evening I distributed among them a case full of knickknacks: red cloths, ribbons, knives, scissors, small mirrors, paints, axes, buttons, bells, and hooks, which they received with indescribable joy. They swore forever to be the faithful sons of their dear father, the Great White Chief. At sunset they departed, recrossing the creek in a southwesterly direction. Kana Hexaya, their chief, is very intelligent. He is about forty-five years old and almost six-and-a-half feet tall. In his warrior's regalia, armed with bows, arrows, quiver and shield, he makes an impressive appearance. His face and hands are painted red and blue, and even his nails are decorated with monsters.

August 23. Since the ground was more or less dried out, we continued about six miles down the creek when we suddenly sighted a great number of squaws (Indian women), as they were digging roots on the banks of the creek. But they noticed us almost at the same moment. They jumped on their horses and rode off with great speed towards their distant village to announce our approach. A few of them, however, not having their horses nearby, could not escape before John, the interpreter, went among them to explain our peaceful intentions. We learned that they were Wichita and that their village was only five miles away. They cordially invited us to visit them, promising a friendly reception. Soon we arrived at the village on the shore of Rush Creek and set up our camp a few hundred paces away, in the valley below.

In no time at all we were surrounded by the inhabitants of the entire village and besieged by questions, such as where had we come from, where were we going, and had we seen any Comanche. According to them, we were the first white men who had ever visited them; very likely they were expecting gifts.

There are two villages here near each other, both peopled by Wichita. The location is well chosen, set in an apparently extremely fertile valley. They raise maize, squash, peas, beans, cucumbers and melons. They do not possess ploughs or other tools for cultivation, using only small hoes. Even so, the fertile soil amply rewards their small efforts; the Indians who cultivate the land never suffer any need.

The village below our camp consists of forty-two huts, in each of which two families reside; only the chiefs have separate huts. If we assume five members in each family, the population comes to about 400. The huts are constructed in the following manner: The heavy ends of many poles are stuck in the ground and evenly spaced to form a circle. Then, starting at the bottom, thin reeds are woven through them and pulled together as they rise upward. On the top, an opening is made just large enough for smoke to escape. A hut and its walls constructed in this manner greatly resembles a cone-shaped Hungarian covering basket.* The sides are then decorated with three to four layers of dried grass tied to the frame with reeds so that the winds will not blow them away. The entire interior of the hut is lined with deerskin and embellished with various figures painted in gaudy colors. All around there are bear- and buffalo-skin couches. In the center of the hut a perpetual fire is burning, and when members of the two

*Used in Hungary to cover leavening bread.

families come together, they lounge around the fire chatting. It is a pleasing sight to a stranger, and it fills the visitor with the joy and satisfaction of contemplating the blessings of domestic happiness. I confess that I did not expect to find this among these people.

The diameter of the huts at the bottom is thirty-five feet without exception; the height, twenty-five feet. From the distance they look like smoking haystacks.

Besides the two villages mentioned, there are three others alongside Rush Creek and two more on Beaver Creek. With the exception of a few bands that roam around between the Wichita Mountains and Canadian River, the entire nation has started to cultivate the land. This is a great gain for civilization, considering that just a few years ago this same Wichita nation caused more fear and anxiety along the borders of the western states than all the other Indian nations combined. Children in Missouri and Arkansas can be silenced to this very day with the single word "Wichita."

I regret to mention, however, that the Wichita still rob and steal when they can, and if they can't, they beg; only fear puts a brake on this evil bent, for they are also cowardly.

Squeezed between the white settlements on one side, and the brave and savage prairie Indians on the other, they depend on the benevolence of these two powerful neighbors. They evidently feel this very deeply, for they constantly assured me that they wished to live in peace and friendship with everyone.

To feed both ourselves and our cattle, I procured from the chief the standing maize crop on a piece of land (about five acres) in exchange for a single-barrel rifle which he wanted. I have had the maize harvested and, after feeding the entire staff for two days, the rest was loaded onto the wagons. When the wagons were full we drove the cattle and mules into the field, where they had a veritable feast.

The second village is only one mile from the first and consists of thirty-five huts built similarly to the ones previously described. The people of the two villages live in perfect peace and harmony.

Buffalo and deer are plentiful in the vicinity, so the Wichita are well provided with venison, and their clothes, bedding, and other household needs, are all made of pelts, like those of the Comanche. I must admit that the Wichita women could compete with any Hungarian tanner in the preparation of skins. Bows and arrows are used for weapons, and sometimes spears and shields for defense. Firearms are

8. *Wichita Village at Rush Creek*, original drawing by Xántus, August 22, 1856; print by Rohn, Pest, 1858.

seldom used, although they can handle them well. I also noticed that they are quite skillful with the simplest flintlock rifle. Their horses and mules are so numerous that they do not even know how many they own. Most of these are of Spanish origin; many have Mexican brands on them, so presumably they were obtained from the prairie Indians in barter. However, we also saw larger horses, which were undoubtedly stolen from Missouri and Arkansas.

To our great astonishment, we heard from the Wichita that in Fort Riley and Fort Arbuckle, the Keechee Indians are spreading the news that our entire expedition was massacred and annihilated by the southern Comanche at the headwaters of the Arkansas. This tale may have been invented by the southern Comanche themselves or the Kiowa, for they are the only Indians who periodically stay in that region. The Keechee and Wichita would never dare to roam so far on the prairie. The details and movements of our expedition described by the Indians, as well as the particulars about our personnel and weapons, are so precise that those who spread the story must have been in our vicinity and carefully observed our every move. This would also explain why they never wanted to meet us, although we saw them several times and often went through their camps, which they had vacated just before we arrived. Presumably they may have thought that we were a military expedition, heading, perhaps, into their country to threaten them because of their pillage and plunder. They may also have thought that the news of our destruction would deter others from coming to our aid.

To-ze-Squas, the Wichita chief, invited all of us, toward evening, to a dance festival and feast to celebrate the corn harvest. Arriving punctually at the prescribed time, we stationed ourselves on high ground, from which we would have a good view. Soon after our arrival the dancers appeared, all of them men. They approached us one by one with great dignity. They all wore knee-length, whimsically shaped skirts; the upper parts of their bodies were completely naked and painted dark red, with varied, thin, circular, yellow and blue designs. White, yellow, and blue painted tassels adorned their bare arms and legs, while their necks were encircled with necklaces of badger teeth, causing ear-splitting noise and clatter with every move. Various gaudy parrot feathers fluttered on the crowns of their heads. In one hand they held a hollowed-out, dry pumpkin, hanging on a string and filled with dry corn kernels and pebbles, which produced an awful, deafeningly

9. *Wichita Maiden,* unsigned

shrill music. In the other hand, strung on a cord, they held all kinds of small corn cakes, which they called *jupellaj*. Their knees and ankles were circled with small turtles, snail shells and antelope claws, while a long fox tail loaded with garish snail shells hung from the back. I must say that the costumes fit the music which every motion of the dancers produced. Opposite the dancers there was also a five-piece orchestra, the musicians dressed in their everyday village clothes. Two of them performed kneeling on the ground and in front of each of them was a huge, dry half-pumpkin, its open end down. Their left hands held a long, smooth stick fitted to the top of the pumpkin, while the right hands held another slotted stick, and drew it back and forth over the smooth one as if they were sawing. This produced a sound that resembled the squeaking of dry grindstone. Such was the music.

The leaps and other motions of the dancers were not very different from the dances of other Indians. I just want to add that the orchestra, beside the aforementioned squeaks, rhythmically tooted and yelled conscientiously and were answered in kind by the dancers. The refrains were joined in with great enthusiasm by the audience, consisting of the entire village population.

At the head of the dancers there were three splendidly costumed old Indians, whose function was to stop before each hut, make a speech, and start the singing. The tune was always and everwhere the same.

Hi to e u, ha ha hi tu, eh u ho ha, ha ha ha, ho ho ho ho! Hi tuh eh ah! tut-t-t-t-tut, tut-t-t-t-tut!

Thus, they went from hut to hut, singing and dancing and they were treated with a variety of corn cakes at each place. We richly shared in the hospitality.

August 24. It rained all night, and it is pouring right now, so we are staying on another day. Early in the morning I sent a message to the two village chiefs asking them to visit me. They were holding two Mexican prisoners and I tried to persuade the chiefs to release them. One of them was a man of about forty, the other a mere boy of fifteen. When the older one was brought to me he told me that he had lived among the Wichita since his childhood and had no wish to leave them. He was as good a horse thief and adventurer as any full-blooded Indian, and he did not believe that he could ever again live at home among civilized people. His words, as well as his entire being, convinced me that he was telling the truth. I did not try to force him to

134

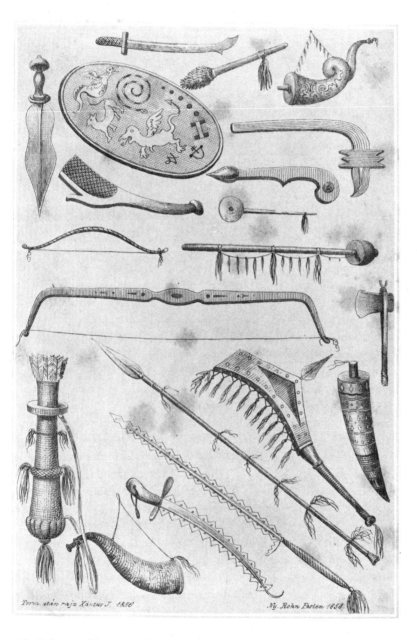

10. *Indian Artifacts*, original drawing by Xántus, 1856; print by Rohn, Pest, 1858.

change his mind. The youth had only been among the Wichita for a few months. He related how a band of pillaging Kiowa stole him from his parents' home in Chihuahua. The Kiowa treated him badly, so he managed to escape. Nearly starving to death, he struggled through the mountains, where the Wichita found him and took him in. He was always treated well by them, but he was quite homesick, and with tears in his eyes he implored me to take him with me. He seems to be an intelligent boy who reads and writes well in his native tongue.

I informed the Indian chiefs that the people of the Union are on friendly terms with the Mexican Republic, and are obligated by treaty to free every Mexican national held by Indians and repatriate them. Also, every effort will be made to put an end to the destruction and banditry carried on so extensively in the northeastern provinces of Mexico.

I further informed the chiefs that the Great White Chief would not be friendly to any Indian nation that did not help to execute and fulfill this treaty obligation. Therefore, he is confident and hopeful that every friendly Indian nation will bear this treaty in mind and place all their Mexican prisoners at his disposal. Having said my piece, I called on them to free and hand over the youth in question, mentioning at the same time that if my request is granted voluntarily I would distribute the gifts that the Great White Father in Washington was sending to all his red children who behave well and show true friendship to his people. They hesitated for a long time, maintaining that the boy belongs to a warrior presently absent who loves him very much and is not likely to let him go with good grace. Upon this I cautioned them once more that if the boy is let go willingly they could expect a reward, otherwise I would use force to free the boy, and no reward or gifts would be forthcoming. The threatening tone of my speech did not fail to achieve the desired effect, for the chiefs announced that I would get the boy provided that the family of the owner would receive some additional reward besides the much anticipated gifts. So I distributed the gifts, and to the family in question I added a pistol and an axe. I took the boy, but first the Wichita completely undressed him, depriving him of all the rags that his clothing consisted of, and threw him naked into my lap. The poor boy burst into joyful tears when I handed him the necessary clothing. (On our return we took up a collection, filled his purse, and sent him on to Fort Riley, from where Major Sibley took him to Texas to be sent on to his parents.)

Before bidding farewell to our Wichita friends, and to continue my diary, I am compiling a few Wichita and Comanche words and

11. *Wichita Dance*, original drawing by Xántus, August 23, 1856; print by Rohn, Pest, 1858.

phrases. Originally I intended to prepare a complete Comanche dictionary, but I cannot afford to do so until I am in more settled circumstances.

English	Comanche	Wichita
blanket	veh nupp	évétirkocs
mirror	nebuni	ecsiuvecs
paint	piszipi	tereuve
tobacco	pehmuh	vejku
gunpowder	nekucsi	itikud
rifle	pilit	ketukes
arrow	paark	nejkvacs
bow	hueeti	kisztiics
yes	hah	ves
no	kejh	kieri
to hear	negut	tuocskes
to sleep	itipi	aszucsazubik
to come	himmeh	tuteos
to go	nebedekeh	teecsocs
battle	hokkuni	vetecsiocskas
to understand	me elo	tocs es
talk, conversation	tekvah	vastakkiza
look here	kebbun	essziesz
I see		unsze es
tell him	marie vittuh	e szok um
he says		tak kasz
how much		acs-kincs
how far is it ?		e szi ke acsi va ?
good, well	cset, cseta	ecstek
bad, badly	tehecsit	neuteh
big	piopp	tocsteh
little, small	tirticsi	kiecsteh
black	tuhup	koras
dead, deadly	tejeh, tejehed	vetetas, vetetase
God, spirit	tarapi	
my father	nerekpi	
my mother	nerbier	
my brother	nerteme	
my sister	nerpecsir	
my son	nertner	
my daughter	nerpeter	
my husband	nerkumegpeh	
my wife	nerkvir	
child	tuecsi	
boy	tuenikpi	

English	Comanche	Wichita
girl	vajepicsi	
face	kuve	
body	vekcsir	
head	peaft	
heart	pihi	
breast, bosom	tuku	
hair	perpi	
hand	mehveh	
thigh	etukuh	
leg	nehepp	
neck	tujok	
eye	necsicse	
mouth, lip	teppah	
tongue	arrakku	
back	kvehi	
bone	szunip	
blood	piszhipeh	
ear	nekerki	
scalp	pahpi	
buffalo	kukcsu	borbucs
ox	pimuru	
horse	tehijji	
deer	null likkeh	maklik
turkey	kujjunitteh	raszvajk
day	tehharp	paszkap
summer	taarcs	
winter	tuhen	
spring	teneheru	
night	tukerreh	
morning	puje erku	
darkness	tcir	
rain	ermer	nagmasz
snow	terkau	
lake, large water	perhep'ia	
prairie	pihiveleti	puszveatuh
spring	pehep, pih	
bread	te esetar	
melon	pihine	kavihin
firewood	kuonih	
forest	huokart	
bird	hucsu	tocseravik
fish	pekveh	
snake	nubi, ir	ecshiriko
stone	terp	
tin	nupparki	

English	Comanche	Wichita
pipe	tujis	tevikele
hut, tent	kehkemih	aszukocse
necklace	csinipp	
kettle, caldron	vejhituveh	
canoe	vuvipoke	
ax	huhimne	
spear	csik	
knife	vith	
flint	nedekurti	
buskin	meepi	
club, mace	vitveh	
village	kinukiju	
warrior	tuavicse	
warmth	ureth	
cold	urcseth	
white	tusup	
red	akupti	
nice, pretty	cserhe bumi	
alive	nejure	
salt, salty	onebitvi	
near	mejtics	
far	menerki	
tomorrow	pearcski	
to kill	mejvejkum	
to eat	tukerru	
to stroll	hirmus	
to run	nokeark	
to drink	hibirtu	
to cry	tejkej	
to lament	kummerpi	
to love	timiehruh	
to exchange	nabuni	
to see	hubiiri	
to sing	niirkir	
to dance	nini	
I, me	hem	
he, him	suku	
thou	hircsi	
they, them	puncsi	
alright	osusu	
perhaps	vuherkini	
man	tujbutszi	subirikics
woman	vajipi	kehaak
white man	tuj ititszi	ikeris

English	Comanche	Wichita
Mexican	tekutibu	isztehi
Negro	tusetajbu	esztehierusku
Indian		chhosz
Delaware		nehrveruh
Kickapoo		sekikehkveh
Cherokee		sannek
Osage	wassese	venseke
Comanche	comanche	natav
chief	tekkvinnuh	areoh
friend	harcs	kincs
foe	tuhubekeh	nautevehe
one		czeos
two		vics
three		tevvej
four		taak vics
five		iszkve ecs
six		hihes
seven		kioffics
eight		kiuteveh
nine		szenkinti
ten		eszkirievecs
horse	puki	kevera
mule	murruh	mohorak
bear	villeh	vierehe
dog	csarli	kitsze
prairie dog	kitszieke	kitszuehe
sun	tearpik	kisev
moon	musi	moar
stars	tearcsi	ekediku
water	peh	kiszi
fire	kunne	isztore
trail		tujeh ecsku
smoke	kuktoe	ecske aszku
running water	ho-no	het
mountain	tujeviszte	nijekauti
maize	henebite	tais
grass, weed	micsizike	ekjekud
tree	chopi	kavk

August 25. At four in the morning we left behind the Wichita village, and it was our intention to follow the Indian trail to Fort Arbuckle. About ten miles further we discovered that our Wichita friends, with their characteristic hospitality, had stolen several articles 141

from one of our wagons, evidently thinking that they could make better use of them than we could. Unfortunately for us and fortunately for our Wichita friends, we had gone too far to turn back to reclaim the stolen articles. Our Spanish boy also affirms that before we left, he was given the fatherly advice to grasp the first opportunity to steal as much as he could, jump on the best horse, and sneak back to their welcoming bosom.

August 26. We saw many buffalo tracks, but not the animals themselves, although we should like to come to grips with them. Toward evening, when we drove the livestock to graze and were about to settle down in comfort, one of our hunters rushed in with the news that he just saw a panther crossing the creek, heading our way. This caused quite a commotion in the camp. In a matter of minutes everybody was up and grabbing their rifles. We all ran together with our dogs to the place indicated by the Delaware. Reaching it, we found fresh tracks in the sand, confirming the nearby presence of the panther. Right then and there we tried everything, even striking them repeatedly, to sick the dogs after the panther. But all our efforts were in vain, for our dogs, instead of sharing our fighting spirit and pursuing the quarry, were more inclined to turn back when their noses sniffed its scent. We were just about to lose heart and give up when John appeared with an old bear-hunting dog which, though aged and infirm, immediately scented the spoor, let out a long wailing howl, and rushed after the tracks. Bravely, he stormed into a thicket, followed by all our dogs, which by now had regained their courage and self-confidence. With loud shouting and yelling we dashed after them. Everyone wanted to be the first to see the panther. Soon the dogs trapped him and, after chasing him around the thicket several times, forced him up a tall poplar. Luckily I was somewhat ahead of my companions; I raised my rifle and dropped him from the tree. The dogs quickly encircled him and my companions greeted him with many bullets. The panther was a truly magnificent animal, nine feet ten inches long and comparatively tall. I promptly had the skin cured and now it adorns my camp stool, in which this diary, sharing my thoughts with you, is written.

August 27. We saw rare and beautiful birds in great numbers and I was fortunate to add to our collection a meadow lark (*Sturnella ludovicacna*), three prairie chickens (*Tetrao cupido*), two bobwhites (*Ortyx virginiana*), and a very rare snipe.

We pitched camp at a small branch of String Creek, in which

there were a few deep ditches filled with vapid water. But hardly an hour passed before our hunters, who were hunting up the creek, rushed back yelling breathlessly, "The water is coming, the water is coming." And sure enough, to our indescribable joy and astonishment, a great deluge roared into the creek bed, filling it completely and even overflowing it in some places. During our entire stay the water kept flowing, as turbid and foaming as at the start. Our Delaware, John, ascribed the event to an indication of favor and good will in which the Great Spirit held us, and from this he divined that our trip would be successful to the end. I cannot explain this phenomenon, because the creek is small, its source is at least six miles from here, and there had been no rain in the last few days, the horizon has been clear all day, clouding over only toward the evening.

There are plenty of strawberries, raspberries, blackberries, as well as wild grapes and plums in these mountains. The grapes are very small but juicy and sweet, and so I believe good wine could be pressed from them. They grow on low bushes just like the gooseberries at home and are found mostly at the water's edge in barren sandy soil. The plum also grows on low bushes about two to four feet high and is wrinkled looking but very sweet. Its color varies from yellow to blood red. Usually it is called *chicasa* prune.

At dawn I sent my friend Hammond to look up the point at which the meridian based on western longitude 100° intersects the southern borderline of Kansas Territory. He rejoined us this evening after carrying out his assignment with precision. The point searched for was a half mile above the Little Verdigris River, on top of an isolated sand dune where a tall poplar stood. The following inscriptions were carved on four sides of the tree: on the north, "Choctaw nation, Kansas Territory, longitude 100°;" on the south "Choctaw nation, Arkansas Territory, longitude 100°;" on the east "meridian of longitude 100°;" and finally on the western side, my name, the day and the year. Besides this, a sealed bottle containing a similar memorandum was buried in a four-foot-deep hole, seven-and-a-half feet from the aforementioned poplar in a direction of 15° NNE.

August 30. In the last few days we sighted pheasants, and mocking birds accompany us everywhere with their sweet singing.

Although its feathers are not particularly attractive and are about the size of an ordinary domestic pigeon, this mocking bird, or many-voiced thrush (*Turdus polyglottus And.*), surpasses the Euro- 143 pean nightingale in every respect because of the inimitable diversity of its melodies. On a clear and quiet night it can be heard at a distance of two to three miles as it imitates with unparalleled fidelity and capricious sauciness the voices of the feathery and mammal animal world. After each imitation it bursts forth with such a hearty chuckle that, willy-nilly, one joins with it. Since I have been in America I have heard hundreds of many-voiced thrushes, but I can truthfully say that I have never heard the same song repeated. No matter how many songs they may sing, each one is more charming and pleasing than the one that preceded it.

September 4. Today we passed over a wide Comanche trail. According to John, these Comanche traveled with their families about two days ago. Therefore, they were on a hunting trip, because when they are on the warpath they leave their families behind and carry as little luggage as possible. On the other hand, when they travel with their families they carry with them all their wordly goods, including tents, frames, and poles, for there is very little wood to be found on the prairie. At such times, they pile all sorts of poles on the horses, the ends of which drag on the ground, leaving behind furrows as if harrowed by a rake. From this one can tell immediately whether the traveling party is hunting or on a warlike expedition. Last year the Comanche manifested hostility toward the Delaware and Shawnee, and although no open warfare has erupted thus far, many were killed in ambush on both sides; and for this reason our hunters are particularly antagonistic toward the Comanche. They are not afraid of them; to my warning that they might meet their enemy when hunting alone, their response was that fear is the least of the worries of the Delaware, even if they were to meet a dozen prairie Indians. It is true that our hunters are brave, skillful and alert lads, and they are armed with six shooters in addition to their bored rifles.

September 5. This morning I rode ahead in the company of two Delaware to reconnoiter the country and to look for drinking water. We had hardly gone three miles eastward when we came upon fresh and warm buffalo tracks pointing to the north. We immediately followed the tracks and soon John sighted the buffalo from a mound. He signaled to us to follow his as he spurred on his horse and sped off. We galloped after him, and when we reached the mound a magnificent sight greeted us. On the flat prairie unfolding before us, about 5,000 alarmed buffalo were madly stampeding, bellowing frightfully.

John galloped about 100 paces behind them, with drawn pistols in both hands. We galloped off the hillside in John's wake. John was on one of our wildest and most headstrong horses, which had never seen a buffalo before. Upon approaching the buffalo, it turned with great fear to the right and left, and reared back in such a way that not one of us could have stayed on it. But no one in our party can compete with John in riding skill. In spite of all the efforts of his mount, John not only stayed in the saddle but rode into the midst of the herd, galloping along while picking off individual ones, firing left and right.

After a headlong dash of five miles, we also caught up with the buffalo, and shot at them constantly for nearly half an hour. At times we were only two to three paces from the terror-stricken animals, but did not kill one of them, although many were so badly wounded that the blood flowed along their flanks. At last one fell, but we left it there and continued firing until finally seven buffalo were on the ground.

By now our horses could hardly trot and the herd left us far behind. We turned back and loaded as many legs of the fallen buffalo as the horses could carry, and we crossed the prairie in a straight line toward the path left behind. Soon we found a spring in a deep hole which I designated as our campsite for tomorrow, and so we returned to yesterday's camp.

In the meantime Hammond followed the Comanche trail for about fifteen miles, where he came upon another of their campsites, but he could not hope to catch up with them because of their two-day head start.

September 6. Today we followed the trail we had reconnoitered yesterday, and when we reached the scene of yesterday's battle, we found hundreds of wolves and thousands of crows feasting on the buffalo carcasses. We did not stop at yesterday's spring but continued through the sparsely wooded prairie to a pleasant-tasting clear creek where we pitched camp. The banks of the creek were covered with many shells and so I named it, Shell Creek.

Among the shells, two species were particularly numerous: *Succiena elongata* and *Helix plebejum*. We collected many of these, and Dr. Baird, the shell expert of the Smithsonian Institution, upon examination, found they greatly resembled those found on the shores of the Rhine, to which Lyell had alluded in his excellent work.*

---

*Sir Charles Lyell, "Fossils, Vertebrates, Fishes, Sharks and their Families Found on the Rhine at Basle," *Proceedings of the Royal Geological Society*, no. 2, 1833–38 (London, 1835): 221–22.

In the evening a few Kickapoo hunters visited our camp. The Kickapoo are all tall strapping lads with an open, straightforward and intelligent expression on their faces, who, with majestic contempt, shun any hint of beggary or submissiveness. The Wichita, however, begged for everything they saw and, in gratitude for the gifts received, stole even more.

September 9. Yesterday we struck an old trail with some faint wagon marks and today we followed it for about eight miles, until we reached a wide and well-defined trail. This was the same road we took last June from Fort Riley to Elk Creek. The entire staff was overjoyed; there was no more need now for pickaxes and spades, for the road had been well prepared, so we piled these tools on the wagons. At nine in the evening we crossed Elk Creek and immediately found ourselves among our friends, whom we found to be in good health. They were very much surprised by our sudden appearance, for vague rumors had convinced them that we had all become victims of the southern Comanche.

I handed over to the chief engineer the column under my command. I must state that the entire personnel performed their duty at all times and under all circumstances with precision, without strife or contention. We did not lose a single man, and our horses and cattle, if anything, were in better shape than when we had started. In fact, we had added three wild horses which we had lassoed as we were roving on the prairie.

1857

S.S. Admiral,
Upper Missouri River
March 9, 1857

As soon as I mailed my letter to you this morning at Fort
Leavenworth, I boarded the steamer and we continued our travel. The
river is jammed with ice floes and the racket is loud enough to make
your hair stand on end, but all this does not bother the American
captain and his passengers, for the desire for gain makes them steam
over ice jams that would terrify a captain on the Danube.

Yet these steamers do not even have the iron hulls of those that
ply the Danube; instead, they are huge wooden castles. Although they
carry 15,000 to 20,000 hundredweight of freight, they steam at no more
than a depth of five feet. I often intended to describe a ship like this,
and now, having sufficient time, I do not want to miss the opportunity
to do so, although our ship is not among the largest that plies the
Missouri. *The Admiral* is 560 feet long and sixty-eight feet wide from
stem to stern and from rail to rail. It has two decks. On the lower deck
are the engine, boilers, firewood, crew's quarters, kitchen, pantry and
partitioned third-class cabins.

The upper deck is completely given over to the first-class
passengers and consists of a long luxuriously furnished salon which   147

runs the entire length of the ship, from which numbered cabins open right and left, each of which is furnished with a small couch, a mirror, and two beds.

Around the entire upper deck there is an open, covered veranda, onto which all cabin doors open and which, at the same time, serves as the entry to the main salon. Along the length of the salon a large table is set for 200 people, at one end of which is a fireplace and a number of smaller tables; at the other end are a ladies' social salon with a piano, two tables, six couches and a fireplace. The anteroom serves as the gentlemen's smoking room, from which three doors open into the common hall.

On the second deck, in comfortable little cabins, live the waiters, ship's officers, servants, chambermaids, helmsmen, and so on.

And above all this there is a small turret-like chamber where the ship's pilot guides the steering wheel.

With all this expensive equipment I thought it impossible for the company to make a profit, but looking into the captain's books, I was convinced of the opposite. For example, on a voyage of sixteen days from St. Louis to Council Bluffs and back *The Admiral* had the following outlay and income:

EXPENSES:

1.	Officers' pay for 16 days	$354
2.	Crew's pay	480
3.	Waiters, servants, porters, etc.	285
4.	480 cords of firewood	1200
5.	Food	150
6.	Insurance	500
7.	Miscellaneous expenses	200
	Total	$3,169

INCOME:

1.	450 passengers—average fare	$3,000
2.	8,000 hundredweight of merchandise, tools, agricultural appliances, etc. from St. Louis to Council Bluffs	6,000
3.	12,000 hundredweight of lead and copper from Council Bluffs to St. Louis	3,000
4.	Small bundles	500
5.	Carrying the mail	600
	Total	$13,100

After deducting expenses from income, a net profit of $10,000 was made on this one trip alone. Taking into consideration the fact that the ship sails along a comparatively sparsely populated area, the cost of transportation for both freight and passengers is fabulously inexpensive, especially in view of the luxury offered the passengers. It is an astonishing achievement.

The American mania for travel is truly hard to understand. Often the ship would stop in a thick forest where one could barely glimpse two or three frame houses, yet twenty to twenty-five passengers would get on or off board. It boggles the mind! Where do they come from, where do they go? Then again the ship would pull up in dense forests, in places where a stranger would swear no one but bears or wolves could live, and there it would unload beautiful velvet and silk-covered furniture, mahogany pianos, and so on.

It is difficult to fathom the American way of life from books and descriptions. You have to roam around and live with them for years to understand and appreciate it. Brome,* in his famous work on America, states that it is no exaggeration to say that at least half the population is constantly on the move. But Brome was here a long time ago. Texas did not yet belong to the Union; Oregon was a British possession; and the inexhaustible gold mines of California had not yet been discovered. Since then speculators have turned toward Kansas and Nicaragua. If Brome were to write an eye-witness account today, undoubtedly he would say that nine-tenths of the American people are constantly on the road.

As soon as an American acquires a few thousand or even a few hundred dollars, he picks himself up and goes west. His baggage seldom consists of anything but a small rubber-lined bag containing a white shirt, a handkerchief, a comb, and a brush. He takes the white shirt in case he may have to make a gala appearance somewhere, or to look respectable in court should he get involved in a lawsuit. On the road all Americans ordinarily wear a red or blue flannel shirt and dark Manchester trousers, which they discard for new ones when they become soiled or worn. All Americans abhor trunks and they are right, for when they arrive in a city they carry everything into the inn or hotel

*This reference is puzzling. There is a 144-page manuscript in the California State Library, "Journal of William Brome on Board the S.S. Nymph," 1852. But it is doubtful that this is the "famous work on America" to which Xántus refers.

themselves and never tip, while the European traveler, if he travels a thousand miles and stops only ten times, would spend at least ten dollars on tips to carry his luggage in and out. Therefore, should the train crash, the ship sink or explode, the hotel catch on fire and burn to cinders, in ten minutes the American will smoke his cigar and smile at the "accident" (as they call every disaster) and calmly go about his business. By the next day he will have forgotten what happened yesterday. He carries everything in his wallet and he cannot lose that unless he himself is lost.

Thus equipped he starts out and travels, for example, on the Missouri River, where right now cities are springing up like mushrooms. Thousands and thousands of people are speculating. Some deal in foodstuffs, some in clothing, and still others build agricultural tools and equipment or found railroad companies. But most of them speculate in land. They pick a location, buy the land from the government, and subdivide it into residential lots. Then in large advertisements they invite the whole world to come and settle there, enumerating the advantages and brilliant commercial future of this booming city (which is as yet only a thick forest or swamp).

These circulars usually include grandiose illustrations depicting railway stations, colleges, hospitals, and other institutions, and are sent all over the states. The masses rush to the new Eldorado.

Once there, a man can seldom turn back, so even though he is deceived and disappointed, he still buys his plot and starts a trade or craft. These towns are almost always founded on the issuance of stock, and it is this stock that forms the basis for the most extensive speculation. For example, today we passed a dozen such towns which are no more than a year old. The founders bought the land at $1.25 an acre and at present (one year later) a residential lot is selling from $150 to $3,000 an acre.

Needless to say many such enterprises go bankrupt, but so many succeed that it is not worth our while to take the former into account.

In order to make full use of Xántus's demonstrated excellence as a naturalist-collector, Professor Baird arranged his transfer from Fort Riley to Fort Tejon in California. Xántus was on his way to Washington to be briefed on his new assignment.

On board the S.S. *Admiral*,
near Lexington
March 10, 1857

A striking example of the American enterprising spirit was exhibited on our ship this morning. As we tied up at Lexington, a very large quantity of whipped butter was offered to us at the fabulously low price of ten cents a pound. I remarked that if anyone could get this butter to Fort Riley he could count on a very nice profit, for butter costs seventy-five cents a pound there. No sooner had I made this observation than I was surrounded by many traveling companions and overwhelmed with questions about my statement. When the ship got under way, some of them were quite ready to undertake the venture. A few were actually prepared to carry out the plan, and after noting down every bit of information and instruction I could give them, they got off the ship in the middle of a forest to return on foot to Lexington. There they will buy up all the butter and tobacco and hire oxcarts to transport it to Fort Riley, where from the proceeds they will buy skins and pelts so that they do not return empty-handed.

They were all convinced that a barrel of butter would bring them $150 net profit.

From Lexington to Fort Riley there is no road, therefore when covering this distance of almost 500 miles with loaded oxcarts, they will have to bridge creeks and rivers, or level their banks in order to proceed. However, the American spirit knows no obstacles whenever there is a prospect for profit.

Such an undertaking in any part of Europe would be the subject of long-lasting discussions, while here it is barely mentioned, except by people who regret they were not the ones to make the $150 profit on a barrel of butter.

Right now we are proceeding through a narrow pass among high mountains. The ice is still drifting, causing considerable damage to *The Admiral;* the fenders of the paddle wheels were lost yesterday; but all this does not hinder its passage. In an hour we shall be in Miami and in three hours in Brunswick [Missouri], where I shall get off, partly because the ship is getting to be so crowded that one can hardly move, and partly because I want to visit my friend Musser.*

*Richard H. Musser of Brunswick, Missouri, was Xántus's lawyer and a newspaper publisher. Musser represented Xántus in his claim for Iowa land and a homestead.

Musser is District Judge of Livingston and also publisher-editor of a political journal, the *Democratic State Gazette*. Besides this he owns a cigar factory and is a soap and candle merchant. He has done much to help the Hungarian cause because of his social prominence and his influential paper.

He is an old, good friend to whom I am obligated for the many gifts he sent to the prairies, which, though small, were always of incalculable value and usefulness to me. He has a lovely, cultured wife and two small daughters whose special favorite I am. Undoubtedly I shall spend a few cheerful and pleasant days with them. This will be most welcome, for by now I have been tramping the western prairies for two years, among wolves, bears, and buffalo, and have had to forego companionship, particularly of the female variety.

Brunswick, Missouri,
March 11, 1857

I arrived safely and landed last night. My friend Musser and his whole family are in Carlton at the court sessions, so I stopped at a hotel. I immediately sent him a telegram announcing that I was here, and by the evening I received an answer saying that he would positively come home that same night. I shall wait for him and most likely will leave for St. Louis on the *S.S. Colonel Chambers* the day after tomorrow.

Brunswick has changed greatly since I was last here. Two years ago there was a big fire here which almost destroyed the town. But, as is often the case, although the fire hurt some individuals, many profited by it.

Before the fire, Brunswick consisted of plank and frame houses built without any plan, and had a population of only a few thousand. At present there are splendid brick and stone houses, the streets are laid at straight angles, and the population has increased to almost 25,000. Four daily and seven weekly journals are published here. There are seventeen churches, a college, a medical school and numerous elementary and Sunday schools.

The post is leaving for the east today, so, for the present, God be with you.

Fort Leavenworth,
Upper Missouri River,
March 12, 1857

Dear Mother:

I wrote you from Fort Riley on the fourth of this month, right after I received your last letter. Soon after that we left and arrived here safely last night. Our trip was romantic in the true sense of the word, as found only in the romances of Sir Walter Scott or the tales of James Fenimore Cooper; but a European can only have a vague conception of it.

We rode close to 400 miles over uninhabited land; at night we pitched our tents and sat around the blazing and crackling fire; and during the ride if one rode ahead or lagged behind and gazed at the company, a more picturesque sight would be hard to imagine. There were 600 Indians accompanying us—about 100 chiefs and 200 prisoners who are on their way to Washington to see the president, to seek remedy for their grievances. These 100 chiefs represent about thirty different nations that inhabit the vast territory between Canada and the Red River, and they are dressed in the most fantastic outfits and armor.

They entertained us at night with their war dances and during the day with their hunting.

It was my intention to write extensively about this trip, but I have just heard the steamer arriving from Council Bluffs, and within the hour we shall be on our way to St. Louis, so I have to close my letter for now. St. Louis is 545 miles from here and we shall be there in about six days. I shall write more fully from there.

The steamer's whistle is sounding, so God be with you.

S.S. *Chambers*,
Glasgow on the Missouri River,
March 13, 1857

Dear Mother:

Yesterday my friend Musser came home with his family and I spent a pleasant day in his house. Last night the packboat from Council Bluffs arrived, and taking advantage of the opportunity I boarded it, continuing my trip to Washington. The name of the packboat is *Colonel*   153

Chambers, and it is similar in every respect to *The Admiral*, which I described in my last letter.

Needless to say, it is an extraordinary spectacle to come upon these floating palaces in the midst of the wilderness. For example, today it is only nine in the morning and we have just met the seventeenth ship to come steaming up the river. These encounters pinpoint for the foreigner how speedily the mail, this most important operation for all Americans, is handled.

The transfer of the mail occurs in the following way. As the ships pass each other at full speed, each captain, without exchanging a word, hurls his mail, which sometimes consists of two to three leather sacks, onto the deck of the passing ship.

I find life on the ship of particular interest. Unlike Europe, on an American ship one cannot buy a passage without meals. Regardless of the distance, food is a *sine qua non*. I think this custom is very sensible, particularly under the prevailing circumstances in America. It could easily happen that someone would book a passage for a thousand miles or longer and be penniless after paying for it. How the dickens would he live for a fortnight? In this way, the passenger cannot become a burden on either the shipping company or his fellow passengers. Having paid for his passage he will be as well provided as a man with thousands of dollars, though he may not have a cent in his pocket.

It is also an American institution that on board ship everyone is treated as an equal except the ladies, who enjoy many extra privileges. Of course it is taken for granted that every courtesy is extended to them.

It is not unusual for fifteen-to-sixteen-year-old girls to travel alone as much as 1,000 miles to visit their father, the only requirement being that they be introduced to and put under the protection of the captain. The father and mother can feel completely secure, for no captain would risk his reputation.

On board ship the ladies are separated at one end of the salon. At the head of the table they also sit separately, and no one can approach them unless the captain introduces him, which he does only after careful consideration, being responsible for the conduct of the person introduced. The ladies, however, can come and go as they please, and it is a surprise to the foreigner to observe the otherwise rough American remove his cigar when the ladies approach, open the door, and close it after them, giving up his seat for them, and so on.

This custom has become so ingrained that it is almost a law by now. It happens often in the Far West when all seats are taken in a stagecoach and a lady wants to get on board at the way station. The last gentleman who got on will give up his seat, get off and wait for the next coach, which sometimes may take a week; or he might have to proceed on foot or horseback. This happens so many times that it does not even occur to the party involved to grumble about it, even though it may be raining hard when he casually gives up his seat as if it were the most natural thing in the world.

The three meals—breakfast, lunch and supper—are almost identical. The American is also very practical in this respect. He cannot see why he should not eat a hearty breakfast when he is just as hungry in the morning as at noon. The American assumes that everybody gets hungry three times a day and remedies his hunger by the same means; and these means are very substantial indeed, unlike the meager samples with which they tease the hungry traveler in Europe.

All meals being the same, I shall describe only one, the breakfast I have just finished. Before doing so, I must state that from five to seven in the morning there is always steaming hot black coffee on one of the tables and the first thing the passenger does after getting up and washing is to sip one or more cups of black coffee; sugar and rum are also on the table and everyone can help himself.

At eight o'clock the table is set and at eight-fifteen the first bell rings; this is the signal to come to the dining room from every part of the ship. Five minutes after the first bell, the officers of the ship escort the ladies to the table and make them comfortable. Meanwhile, the gentlemen stand alongside the long table behind their chairs. At last the second bell rings, signalling to the men to take their seats, which happens with astonishing alacrity, within seconds; and in the next minute the sound of eating can be heard.

Soup is never served and napkins are not used at all in America, nor do they change plates, but everyone eats as much as he likes from the same plate. The table is jam full of large dishes, which are kept warm by the flames of spirit lamps under them. Steaming stews, roasts, pâtés, and so on, are placed on the long table in lavish quantity, as well as compotes, salads, and different kinds of greens; escargots, crabs, oysters, pastry, and fruit are not missing either. In short, few Parisian hotel kitchens could provide all the dishes offered on the ship's table.

Everybody serves himself. There are waiters who stand behind   155 the guests, but only to help when the desired food is not within reach, in which case the plate is handed to the waiter.

On the American table there is no systematic sequence of items on the menu. One person may start breakfast with a salad, another with dessert, a third with crab and venison, still another with almonds or nuts; and by the time a passenger has finished his meal, he has eaten everything spread before him in haphazard order. This whole operation takes a matter of minutes, because the speed of the American eating mechanism is surpassed only by the American steam engine.

Except at regular meal times, no food can be obtained from the kitchen, but drinks, cigars, tobacco, and playing cards can be had at exorbitant prices at any time by asking a waiter.

Lunch is served at two and supper at nine o'clock. After the table is cleared away, there is usually a concert or dance which lasts until well after midnight, for there is always a passenger ready to entertain at the piano, or one who can sing, and there is never a shortage of dancers; and so the ship is noisy from night till morning. The American is not concerned about people who are unable to sleep, for he thinks no one should travel on a ship who cannot sleep amid noise.

We just passed the steamer *Lucy*, which ran aground, and for the past two days has been trying to break loose from the sandbar. Passengers and freight were taken off to the forest to lighten the load. The passengers camped around big fires and exchanged jocular remarks with us as we passed.

By tonight we will be in Jefferson City and by tomorrow at the mouth of the Missouri, from where it is only a few hours' journey to St. Louis. It will be difficult for me to write from St. Louis, for I intend to take the train straight to Washington. My next letter will come from the capital of the Union. The dinner bell is ringing. I must hurry lest the Americans gobble up everything before I get there.

Washington,
March 21, 1857

Dear Mother:

I hope you received my letters written this month from Fort Leavenworth and the steamer *Admiral*; then from Brunswick, and finally from the steamer *Chambers*, I described in detail my journey as far as St. Louis, where I personally mailed my last letter. I spent only two hours in St. Louis—just long enough to transfer my luggage from the steamer to the train and shake hands with a few friends—and I was already racing through the prairies of Illinois. The fare from St. Louis to Washington is only $26.60, which is truly not very much, considering that one gets three good meals a day and sleeps through the night in a comfortable coach, and travels 835 miles in fifty-two hours.

Traveling at such speed prevents me from describing it in detail, and although we passed through such great cities as Terre Haute, Indianapolis, Dayton, Xenia, Columbus, Wheeling, Cumberland, and Baltimore, the whole panorama has a hazy, dreamlike quality in my memory.

Unquestionably the part from Wheeling to Cumberland was the most interesting. At Wheeling we crossed the Ohio River, and soon after our engine pulled us up to a high plateau. Higher and higher we kept climbing, until at last we reached an elevation of 9,400 feet on the ridge of the snow-covered Allegheny Mountains.*

Smilingly, I recalled the lack of enterprising spirit of my poor homeland, when a few years ago it was not considered practical to build the railroad to Fiume because it had to go through the Zagoria Mountains. Finally it was decided that the project was feasible, but only with horsepower.

Let us see how this American railroad came into existence. The idea of connecting Baltimore and the Ohio River occurred in 1848, the same year the company was founded.** The following year, construction began simultaneously at twenty different locations. In June 1856, eight years later, the first train arrived in Pittsburgh from Baltimore; thus, the eighth wonder of the world in communication came into being. The entire system, including the buildings, costs about $73 million (about 150 million florins), and it is already earning 15 percent net profit. From sea level to the top of the snowy mountains, the railroad rises 146 feet for every mile, and from there to Cumberland it descends 154 feet per mile. In many places the road runs from one side of the mountain to the other over ravines hundreds of yards deep, bridged by

---

*Nine thousand four hundred feet is a gross exaggeration. The highest point in the Alleghenies is 4,900 feet.

**Probably the Baltimore and Ohio Railroad but if so, Xántus has the date wrong. It was chartered in 1827.

colossal viaducts which rest on 300- to 400-foot-high granite columns. The engine rushes with dizzying speed toward the stone walls, and everyone thinks that his last hour is at hand and the train will be smashed to bits. Another minute and it is pitch dark; we are in a tunnel and enveloped by a fusty smell, and so for ten to fifteen minutes, often even for thirty, the train speeds through the bowels of the mountain. Then the roar of the waterfalls, the rumble of the rushing mountain streams in every direction, the vast ice fields, and the mining towns, so overwhelm the traveler that he does not know whether to admire the grandeur of nature or that of human ingenuity and enterprise.

The American believes that should the train derail, or in case of any kind of accident, he has little chance to escape, no matter in what nook or cranny of the coach he might be. Accordingly, there are open seats in the coaches protected by wire grills to prevent the passengers from falling out. In Europe this would not be tolerated, but here everyone is thought of as having reached his majority; therefore, one is expected to exercise proper care and to protect oneself. If you take into account that the train climbs up the snowy mountain at the rate of twenty-eight miles an hour and descends at thirty-eight, from an altitude of 10,000 feet, amidst gaping chasms, waterfalls, and steep rock walls, you can well imagine what a breakneck undertaking this trip is. Still, many men and even some women sit in the open seats on top of the coaches, enjoying themselves immensely. They sit in comfort, smoking cigars and telling jokes; it does not even occur to them that their existence may hang on less than a thread. In many places the train runs over precipices on suspension bridges, and although it slows down at such times, the bridge nonetheless sways from left to right, so that one has to hold on to the grill in order not to fall out.

At eight o'clock in the morning, at two in the afternoon and at nine in the evening the train stops at regular stations where tables are set for the passengers and where they may eat and drink for ten minutes. During the same ten minutes, the train is serviced with coal and water, so as not to waste time during the rest of the day. After eight minutes the bell rings and keeps ringing for two minutes, after which time the train always starts promptly, regardless of the passengers. It never stops at small stations, but should anyone want to get on or off, the engine slows down so that the passenger may jump off or on. The mail sacks are also thrown on the run by the conductor at the stations, and the parcels to be forwarded are picked up in the same manner. A European cannot conceive of this. It must be seen to be believed.

I arrived safely the night before last and took lodgings at the Willard Hotel. Yesterday I paid my respects to the secretary of the interior and the secretary of state, Cass, who received me with cordiality and informed me that I have the choice of joining the corps of topographers who will start their activities in Oregon this summer, or of going to southern California to join the mapping party stationed there. I have not yet decided, but I will probably choose California, partly because it is one of the most charming places in the world (no winter, eternal spring) and partly because my position there would be a permanent one, and consequently, since I cannot go home, I might finally settle down there, and on the basis of my present position, I might even get married. It is true, dear mother, that this step would put another 3,000 miles of distance between us, but what can we do? Since fate separated us, let us take advantage of the best it offers. It is also true that correspondence will be more difficult from now on, for the mail from southern California to New York goes only once a month, and takes twenty-two days from San Diego to New York. So at best it will take my letter two months to reach you. No matter, I shall write more and longer letters and I shall expect you to follow my example; let us try to have every mail bring a letter from you and one from me to you.

Tomorrow morning I shall be presented to the new president, as well as to the secretary of war. The result—rather the event—I shall not fail to relate to you in detail.

I learned to my great satisfaction that all of my five compatriots living in Washington are highly respected and are comfortably well off. All of my friends had shared with me many a bitter cup of deprivation and misery in London. Alex Straus is chief of the Bureau of Hydrography with a yearly salary of $2,000; Charles Scholcz is a draftsman at the Maritime Engineering Corps and earns $1,800 annually; Michael Szabo (from Temes) is one of the more important booksellers in Washington; and John Lulay (from Marmaros) is the owner of one of the most elegant furniture stores. All five of them got married during the last year; their wives are all from the same family, and they are all wealthy. When I mentioned this yesterday to old General Cass, he warmly shook my hands and remarked that America would be twice as great if immigration from Hungary would be as extensive as from other nations. This pleased us very much.

Poor and penniless, we arrived in the new world. Without friends, hardly in command of the language, and unacquainted with its customs, we stepped into the arena to compete with the greatest people of the world, and the time needed to acquire citizenship had barely passed when all of us (poor fugitives not long before) achieved independent and distinguished positions of which we are truly proud. Our friends at home may look upon us with gratification, for we have brought honor to our former, beloved country.

Willard Hotel,
Washington
March 22, 1857, evening

Dear Mother:

This noon I was privileged to be presented to the president of the United States of America. Such an event, however, is a most ordinary one in America. The president receives visitors every day, except when there is a cabinet meeting. When someone wishes to speak to the president, he applies to the secretary, who registers his name in a book and escorts him into an anteroom where he must wait his turn. I hardly waited half an hour when the doorman called my name and flung open the wide doors, and without any further ceremony I found myself face to face with the world's greatest elected official. James Buchanan, the recently elected president, is close to seventy years old; he is tall and slender, with an amiable mien. He is completely gray, with long, sparse locks on his head. He was dressed in a long black coat, black trousers, and a white vest, without any ornaments. The spacious reception room is covered with carpeting of fine quality and furnished with a number of chairs and couches of red and dark blue Moroccan leather, with three small, round tables in the center.

Senator Caleb Cushing, with a brief remark, introduced me to the old gentleman, who bowed, shook my hand and offered me a chair. He himself sat down on a couch. He addressed many questions to me concerning the mineral deposits of the Kansas and Arkansas River regions. Then he asked if my parents, brothers or sisters were alive, where they lived and in what circumstances. Then he asked a few questions about the events of the 1840s and finally where K [Kossuth] is at the present time.

The entire conversation took about fifteen minutes, after which he declared how glad he was of my visit and said that should I at anytime need his assistance to carry out my plans, I could turn to him with confidence. He then asked me to sign my name in the visitors' book, after which he again bowed and shook hands and I left.

I was followed by the Sardinian envoy, then by a farmer from Michigan. The antechamber was filled with people from every walk of life. Every American citizen believes that it is his right to visit the official elected by him to the highest office and, when he goes to Washington, to shake hands with him. One can appear on these occasions dressed in any kind of clothing; even gloves are not required.

In addition to these visits the president holds a weekly reception, when the diplomatic corps, the Supreme Court, members of the Senate and the House and the highest-ranking officers of the army and navy pay their respects. On these occasions everyone is expected to appear in dress uniform, or in the choicest civilian clothing.

The president usually entertains every night, but only a few personal friends are invited. Every Friday night there is a *soirée* open to the public, where anyone may appear who is a "gentleman," but it is proper to come after eight o'clock and to leave by ten. The present president is a bachelor and the one who performs the honor of the first lady is his sister, Miss Lane, who is commonly known to be a polite and charming hostess, though a spinster. It is customary to address the president as "Mr. President" and his wife is simply called "Madame."

The president's residence is at the end of Pennsylvania Avenue opposite the Capitol, about one mile from it in the center of a beautiful park. Although built of white marble in excellent taste, it is nevertheless a simple, unpretentious, one storied republican residence, consisting of two large salons and twenty-two rooms, each furnished with simple good taste.

Beside his personal servants, there is no one attending the president, and anyone at any hour of the day may enter the house, park, and inspect anything he wishes. It happens more than once that a visitor may join the president in a stroll in the park.

In this same park is the bronze equestrian statue of General Jackson on a white American marble base. The statue is interesting mostly because of the rearing posture of the horse. The entire and enormous weight rests without any other support on the hind legs. This original concept displays the unparalleled genius of the sculptor, Clarke Mills.

East of the presidential residence, behind Lafayette Square,   161 there is another Leviathan worth mentioning, the federal treasury building, or in European parlance, the ministry of finance. The all-white marble structure is 740 feet long with a wing on the north side. There is another wing to be built on the south side, but as yet only the foundation is laid. The next project is to build up the west side parallel with the frontage, thus forming a huge quadrangle. The facade was built in the form of Athene Minerva's temple of antiquity, with a magnificent colonnade running the entire length.

At present the Federal Land Register occupies the top floor, but soon it will move into a beautiful building of its own on the bank of the Potomac.

Near the presidential residence in the center of Union Park there is an observatory, which, like all public buildings in Washington, is also built of white marble. Undoubtedly it is unsurpassed in the whole world, both from the standpoint of architectural excellence and that of the quality of its instruments.

This institute is under the direction of the world famous mariner, Maury.* Among its unique and notable instruments are a *circulus muralis*, a meridian transit,** and a huge transit to determine the orbits of the stars; then again, there is the prime-vertical transit to explore and measure the refraction of circles, which is Maury's most important invention, and, finally, the truly gigantic equatorial telescope.

The many naval officers who are employed in the various departments show the visitors all these instruments with gracious cordiality. They explain their function and even allow them to be used when they themselves are not engaged in scientific research. The institute building is in the shape of a cross, in the center of which is a high cupola, on top of which there is a 150-foot-high mast. Every day at noon, a huge, red globe ascends to the top of the mast, showing the correct time.

---

*Matthew Fontaine Maury (1806–1873), hydrographer and naval officer. Head of the Depot of Charts and Instruments (1842), later the U.S. Naval Observatory and Hydrographical Office. His *Physical Geography of the Sea* (1855) was the first classic work of modern oceanography.

**The Meridian transit, the modern version of which is called the Meridian circle, is a telescope-type instrument to observe the movement of the stars as they cross the meridian. It is also used to determine time. It operates by recording electrical impulses. The *Circulus muralis*, literally translated, circular mirror, is a navigational instrument also used in astronomy.

Washington,
March 23, 1857

Dear Mother:

At two this afternoon I made a pilgrimage to Mount Vernon, the former residence of Washington, where his remains are laid to rest. My five friends (whom I mentioned in my letter yesterday) and their wives were kind enough to join me, and we took the excursion steamer down the Potomac together.

When I visited this revered place years ago I did not describe it, so now I will tell you a little more about it. Mount Vernon is on the Virginia side of the Potomac, about fifteen miles from Washington, and it still belongs to the Washington family. Every morning a steamer takes visitors there and returns them in the afternoon.

Mount Vernon is amply blessed by nature, and it is the consensus that no country estate on the Potomac surpasses its picturesque beauty. The residence itself is a simple single-story frame house, ninety-six feet long with a wide portico running its entire length. The inner structure and the furnishings are just like they were in Washington's day, and everything is maintained with such conscientious reverence that it is claimed that when Lafayette last visited it in 1824, he remarked to Lavasseur, "Truly, every nail is as it was 30 years ago."

Among others, the large key of the "Bastille," which Washington himself hung on a nail above the window, is still hanging there and has never been touched by another hand. Scattered all over his study are his books and clothes, and in general the entire room reminds one of the great man. In this same room there is a book, into which every visitor gladly signs his name.

Winding garden paths lead to a lovely hill to the north. Reaching its top, the pilgrim is suddenly confronted with the grave, amidst rich cypress and magnolia trees. The remains of the world's greatest figure lie in a simple, white marble sarcophagus. The American emblem is carved on the front and underneath it are just the two words, *George Washington*. Next to it is an almost identical grave with the simple inscription, *Martha Washington*.

It is customary for visitors to take as a memento a small branch of cypress surrounding the grave, as well as some of the plants on it. Just as I had done a few years ago, I again faithfully performed this act, and am sending these souvenirs home to my friends.

I think they will appreciate it, for I could hardly send in a letter anything more valuable than a cypress branch from Washington's grave.

To demonstrate the reverence in which Washington's memory is held, whenever a steamer passes by the grave, a black flag is hoisted and the bell is sounded; and when a warship approaches on the Potomac, the entire crew line up on the deck, present arms and salute the flag at half-mast.

March 24, morning

I interrupted my letter because my nieces (my friends' wives) came for me and took me with them. Truly my life here is so much fun and only one who has been a refugee can appreciate it. The little women took it into their heads to call me "Uncle John," and, in consequence, I call Lily, Nancy and the others, my nieces. In view of this relationship, I demanded the rights of a kissing cousin, which were agreed to without dissent. The ladies pranced around me in a circle, treated me as a little old uncle, and were greatly amused at my expense.

Involuntarily one would think of them as Hungarian ladies, for all of them always refer to themselves as "we Hungarians." They would love to marry me off so the company would be an even half dozen.

The husbands are serious fellows, yet last night we almost burst with laughter, playing post office, chasing each other around, dancing the *csárdás*, and singing folk songs; in short, we made enough racket to prevent our poor neighbors from sleeping.

The clerk of the secretary of interior just arrived with a message that I should report at once to his office. Probably they have made a decision about my future post. I will rush off now, but as soon as I return I shall let you know the results.

March 24, noon

Dear Mother:

I have just returned from the secretary of the interior and hasten to inform you that upon his urgent recommendation I have accepted the California engagement. On the sixth of next month (eleven days from now), a steam frigate is leaving New York. I shall travel on it to Chagres,* from there to Panama by rail, and from Panama to San Francisco (the capital of California) on one of the ships of the Pacific Steamship Company. From San Francisco we shall travel on muleback to the Tejon Mountains, together with a topographical staff which we are to recruit in San Francisco.

This post on the Pacific was just established and its task is to map the topography of all of southern California, Sonora, the Gulf of California, and the Mesilla Territory.

This, of course, will take several years, and so I have a secure and permanent position as long as I want it. We are authorized to build permanent headquarters for the surveying party in the Tejon mountain pass, and the government will run a monthly mail service between us and San Francisco.

This being a region where practically no one has been before, you can count on me for interesting descriptions and sketches.

Your letters, however, should be addressed to Brunswick until further notice.

Tomorrow afternoon I shall go to Philadelphia, where I intend to spend a few days with my friends, and I shall also visit Samuel Ludwigh in Baltimore. On the second of next month I shall go from Philadelphia to New York, and on the third I am to report to the captain of the frigate.

Fossards Hotel,
Philadelphia, Pennsylvania,
March 29, 1857

Dear Mother:

I hope you have received my last letter from Washington, in which I informed you about obtaining a position in California with a survey party to be organized there. I also told you of my anticipated departure from New York on April 6, so by the time you receive this note I shall be riding the waves of the Pacific Ocean.

On March 24 at noon I left Washington, after bidding good-bye

*Present day Colón in Panama.

to my friends, two of whom accompanied me on the train to Baltimore. There I wanted to visit Samuel Ludwigh to greet him at least, but he was not at home, having gone to Savannah to lecture against the temperance societies there. Our friend Sam is a mighty and much feared exponent in this field. His wife was at the theater, and thinking that she might have insisted on my staying over, and not quite trusting my ability to say no to a lady, I returned to the railroad station with my baggage and took the next train to Philadelphia, where I arrived safely at noon on March 25.

I had many old friends here whom I had gotten to know through correspondence only. It was all the more gratifying to make their personal acquaintance now. For a long time I have been a member of the Academy of Natural Sciences here, and so yesterday I made my acceptance speech at their monthly session. I am being recommended now for corresponding membership in the Philosophical Society, the Society of Natural Sciences and the Franklin Society, and I will no doubt be elected.*

Philadelphia is certainly the most beautiful city in the Union. Its population is not larger than that of Vienna, but it is at least four times the size. The quality of its public buildings surpasses anything I have seen so far in America.

The mobility and style of life can by judged by one who is acquainted with the local conditions. No other city has more charitable institutions, and most of its 218 churches are masterpieces of architecture.

The entire city is well paved. The sidewalks are eighteen feet wide and paved with white stone. All the streets are lined with tall trees, which are teeming with thousands of squirrels so tame that they eat the nuts out of your hand. The public squares are all made into parks, each with its own little lakes where swans and ducks swim.

It is almost miraculous for an industrial and commercial city to be so spotlessly clean, and I was impressed with the good appearance of the people I met on the streets. Even the elderly ladies are generally attractive. One will not find the fiery beauty of the Italians or that of the marble-like British, but something of a mixture, which is very characteristic.

Anyone going to Philadelphia should not fail to be recom-

---

*Xántus was elected to the Academy of Natural Sciences, but he was never a member of the American Philosophical Society.

mended to Madame Rush. I was presented to her today and must say that I have never seen so many beautiful women gathered together in one place.

Madame Rush is a wealthy banker's wife who runs a princely house, a beautiful garden, a picture gallery, and a sculpture collection. She holds a reception every Sunday morning, which all of Philadelphia's high society attend, for there are always famous musicians, singers and foreign guests present.

These matinées resemble the Parisian "reunions," except that here they end with an elaborate breakfast equal to a full-scale midday meal. On this occasion I was pleasantly surprised by the great selection of Hungarian wines from Somla, Tokai, Buda, Magyarád, plus sparkling wine from Poxsony.

I was told that in recent years a great deal of Hungarian wine has been consumed by the wealthy, a fact of which I was unaware. Later I have found on restaurant menus lists of Hungarian wines, and I can report that a bottle of Somlai costs three dollars, Tokai, four dollars and red Buda, two-and-a-half dollars. You can imagine the profit the merchants make, but I do not begrudge it, for they are spreading the fame of our country's wines.

Of the twenty-one theaters only three are open now, winter being the regular season: one burlesque house, another for drama, and one Italian opera. In this last I saw, or rather heard, *The Barber of Seville* last night. The chorus was particularly good.

There are many things of interest in Philadelphia and I regret that I cannot acquaint you with all of them, though not for selfish reasons, for I should love to share my experiences with you, but my limited time at present does not permit it.

Perhaps in one of my future letters I shall return to the subject of Philadelphia. But right now I have so many things to do that with the best of intentions I cannot find the time. I have a great deal of shopping to do for articles which are either unavailable or too costly in California. The long time I have spent on the western prairies has taught me that sometimes the possession of small things can make all the difference between comfort and hardship.

It gives me particular satisfaction to comply with mother's old wish, and at last I had two photographs taken of me today which I am sending with Wilhelm Rosenthal, a German forwarder who guaranteed to deliver them to you. I am sending one to Gyula and the other to Mali, because mother is staying with one or the other, so there is no 167 need for an extra one. If I have time enough in San Francisco I shall have one painted of me and will then send a third.

Needless to say I should be very happy if I could have a picture of all of you.

New York,
April 2, 1857

Dear Mother:

A few days ago I wrote to you from Philadelphia that I am going to New York. I left Philadelphia yesterday morning and traveled on a steamer on the Delaware as far as Amboy. I did this only to see the river, for it would have taken less time by rail. The Delaware is one of America's most delightful rivers. It is teeming with life, with sailboats and steamers everywhere. Lovely villas and parks smile on the traveler from the shores. These villas are built in the most fantastic styles. Most of them are semi-gothic and semi-moorish, with numerous turrets, which lend a peculiar character to the entire landscape.

At the mouth of the Delaware at Amboy I took the train, and at seven in the evening I took up lodgings at the Taissant Hotel in New York.

New York has also changed a great deal since I was here last. Many main thoroughfares were already very grand, but much has been demolished and replaced by marble palaces. Fourth and Fifth Avenues, in my opinion, surpass in magnificence any street of Paris or London.

This morning I visited the ship on which I plan to travel. It is truly a huge floating castle. Its name is *Illinois*, in honor of the state of the same name. Monday morning at seven, God willing, we shall leave and travel through the West Indies to Chagres, from Chagres to Panama by train, and from there to San Francisco by a steamer of the Pacific Railroad Company.

If everything goes well we shall complete this trip in twenty-two days. Although we shall disembark in Panama, forgive me, mother, if I do not write from there, for transferring from ship to train and six hours later from train to another ship makes it impossible even to think about writing. However, as soon as I reach San Francisco I shall write in detail.

12. *Union Square, New York*, unsigned; print by Rohn, Pest 1858.

San Francisco, California
May 1, 1857

Dear Mother!

I hasten to inform you that after a twenty-four day voyage I arrived last night safely and in good health.

As I wrote to you from New York in my letter of April 2, we were to sail April 6, and on schedule at seven-thirty in the morning the *Illinois* left with 1,246 passengers (342 women and 216 children among them). On the eighth we passed Cape Hatteras, and on April 10 the Bahama Islands. On the twelfth, which was Easter Sunday, we sailed under the huge rock cliffs of Santo Domingo in a southwesterly direction. At nine o'clock in the morning of April 13, the Jamaican pilot climbed on board, tied his schooner to our side, and by noon he had brought us to the island of Jamaica. By one-thirty in the afternoon we were at Port Royal, and a half an hour later we reached the capital of Jamaica, Kingston, where we took on coal and fresh water. Taking advantage of the six hours in port, we went ashore to look over the city.

The population of Kingston is about 25,000, and it has many churches, a university, a library, and some scientific institutions. It also has 109 sugar mills and over 100 rum distilleries. The cost of a bottle of rum in Hungarian currency is ten cents; one pound of sugar costs two cents; a pineapple, one cent; a dozen oranges, three cents; a dozen lemons, five cents; and a pint-and-a-half of coffee, two-and-a-half cents.

There are very few cattle on the island, and accordingly beef is very expensive, but sheep and goats are all the more abundant; millions of them graze on the mountain sides. The cost of a sheep is thirty cents and of a goat, fifteen cents. The largest part of the population is Negro, mulatto, quadroon and sambo; they rush to and fro half-naked, their only cover an apron and a straw hat. The white population consists solely of English soldiers, officers, merchants, consuls, and government employees.

The city is completely hidden among the mountains and it is literally invisible until one is actually on its streets. There are two islands and a peninsula that juts into the sea directly in front of it, both heavily fortified and armed with powerful cannons. The entire bay is filled with English warships.

The evening of the thirteenth we raised anchor and steamed on the calm seas, but not for long this time, for by the morning of the fifteenth we sighted the South American coast. We steamed by New Granada and by one-thirty in the afternoon we arrived at Chagres, where we tied up at the port. The port is excellent, because the sea is very deep, so that the heaviest ships can tie up at the shore. Chagres at the present time is almost completely in ruins; hardly anyone lives there, but directly opposite it a new city named Aspinwall* has been under construction for the past two years; it is flourishing and a train goes from it to Panama. We also visited this city, and since the train was not scheduled to leave until five in the afternoon, we had enough time to inspect the city. It already has a population of 10,000, although only two years ago it was a virgin forest, and is built on an unhealthy undergrowth.

The mixture of color and nationality in the population suprasses anything I have seen in my life.

Millionaires and adventurers gather here for one purpose only— to accumulate money. There is hardly a language in the world which is not heard. From the north to the south pole all produce and goods are concentrated here because it is a starting point—eastward to Europe, northward to the United States, Mexico, Central America, the West Indies, South America and Africa, and lastly, westward to Japan, China, the Sandwich and Tahiti Islands, Australia, New Zealand, and East India.

Owing to its location, there is no question that Aspinwall has a great future, and it is not impossible, as many claim, that in a quarter of a century it will be one of the most important cities in the civilized world. It is also the meeting place of freebooters, who form all kinds of companies to make their fortune.

There are so many desperadoes here that any plan or scheme will find an echo and backers with sufficient funds to equip an expedition to explore this or that island, to search for gold mines, or to conquer and subdue any land.

Right now John Aspinwall (the founder of the city and a New York banker) is building a warehouse of carved granite at the port. It is going to be nearly three-fourths of a mile long with eight stories and will be proportionately deep. When I was there, 1,700 laborers, not including the stonemasons, were working on it. If one considers that a common laborer gets four dollars and free board a day, one can imagine

---

*The old city of Chagres and the new city of Aspinwall are the present-day Colón.

how much this building is going to cost and what a huge volume of business is anticipated for the enterprise.

At five in the afternoon we finally boarded our train and penetrated the vast forest, which is the primeval home of tigers, panthers, bears, and boas. The isthmus between Aspinwall and Panama is forty-one miles long but the railroad is sixty-eight miles long, because it is not possible for it to cross the sky-high Cordilleras in a straight line.

It is with amazement and astonishment that one views this miracle of the century, this triumph of civilization and enterprising spirit. Only a few short years ago this was an impenetrable jungle, full of wild and bloodthirsty animals and boas. It took ten to twelve days of terrifying struggle to get through to the Pacific Ocean, during which time the adventurous traveler was subjected to frightful hazards, and now the steam engine transports the passenger in comfort. He can sit back on morocco and velvet chairs smoking a Havana cigar, and admire the lush tropical vegetation.

The train runs on tracks cut into the mountainside and there are only four tunnels on the entire line. The run is a succession of twisting spirals.

On account of the numerous swift mountain streams, it was necessary to build many bridges. During the rainy season, the overflow that rushes down from the mountains obstructs the tracks with its débris, and a crew of laborers is needed all the time to clear them. For this purpose the company maintains a depot every ten miles, where the supervisory personnel oversee the maintainance crew.

At the same time these depots constitute the vanguard of civilization, for around each one a little town has been built, which serves as the market center for the produce and labor of the area. Within a few years civilization will take root, replacing the monkeys and parrots, which, as though aware of the future, make the most unholy racket as the train moves on. One can hardly hear one's own voice.

It also happens sometimes that the monkeys attack the engine with oranges and lemons. At such times, one or another of the passengers will fire a shot among these revolutionaries, who quite sensibly turn tail and vanish into the jungle.

172   To describe or sketch the flora under these tropical skies is

beyond human ability. I have read a great deal about South America and have seen the masterpieces of many an artist, but now that fortune has favored me with the chance to see it all in person, I must smile with indulgence at even Humboldt and Velasquez. Here and there, jungles intertwined with impenetrable vines and towering peaks of 10,000 to 12,000 feet stretching toward the sky in the most fantastic shapes; there are also lakes, rushing creeks, and dense forests of mahogany.

There are thousands and thousands of trees and vines, and species of flowers we have never before seen. Everything is so new and so beautiful, surpassing anything one could dream of. There are 150-foot-high yellow, red and blue oleanders, magnolias with huge white flowers, and hundreds and hundreds of varieties of tall palms, weighted down with the heavy burden of a variety of fruits. The riotous magnificence of all this color can be remembered but not adequately described.

The train passed by several settlements and we could observe the natives sitting in front of their huts in unmistakable contentment. The men were almost naked, while the women—all attractive—were dressed in spotlessly clean, long white gowns. They all wore wide-brimmed straw hats with a hole cut in the top for the free circulation of air, which I think is an ingenious invention.

At any rate they are past masters in weaving straw hats and they are recognized as such, for Panama hats are already as famous and costly in America as the florentines* are in Europe. Although a good and durable straw hat can be bought here for one dollar, a top quality hat would cost forty to sixty dollars. They can, however, be worn for many years, washed many times and, if folded and pocketed, will not break.

Around eight o'clock in the evening, the Pacific Ocean appeared before us like a huge mirror, and in a few minutes we were on its shore in the harbor of Panama. The town is an old Spanish settlement walled on all sides by four towers, one on each corner, well armed and defended by Canadian soldiers.

The population of the town consists of 5,000 Spanish-speaking whites, 1,000 whites of assorted nationalities, and 10,000 coloreds. There is a very nice cathedral built in archaic style, which is the seat of the Catholic diocese of New Granada.

---

*Child's close-fitting hat.

The harbor is very poor, for the water is shallow as far as two miles from the shore; large ships have to drop anchor this far and transport passengers and goods by lighters. During our stay there were an English ship, two French frigates, one Peruvian and one Chilean frigate, two American sloops and in addition, fifty merchant ships of all sizes.

The entire shore is covered with coconut palms, and, with the high Cordilleras in the background, and no other vegetation, the area has a distinctive appearance.

Soon after our arrival we were taken to our ship on small barges which had been waiting for us six miles away, anchored between two islands. It was way past midnight by the time all the passengers and the baggage were on board; outside of those on the *Illinois*, 350 new voyagers joined us. They had arrived from New Orleans, Havana, and Lima the day before, and their destination was also California.

On April 16 at ten in the morning, driven by both sail and steam, we left with 1,596 passengers all told. By the afternoon the shore disappeared on the eastern horizon and we were bucking the high seas. Our ship, the *Golden Gate*, weighs 3,500 tons, is driven by two engines of 500 horsepower each, and the captain's name is Landrum.

On April 17 at noon we were at northern latitude 7° 35′ and western longitude 82° 52′ and on the 18th north latitude 9° 38′ and western longitude 86° 42′. On the same day countless numbers of giant turtles, whales and sharks surrounded the ship. The whales and sharks are still following us, but the turtles we saw only in the harbor.

On the morning of April 21 we reached the Mexican shores, and following it closely all day long, we arrived at Acapulco at five in the evening, where we took on oxen, coal, and water.

The city is not large but is beautifully located. The air is healthy and very clean. The harbor is very spacious and protected by a massively built and heavily armed fortress. Outside of a Mexican warship, there were no other ships worth mentioning in the harbor, although more than 100 schooners were loading and unloading; but they were just taking care of local business.

As soon as we arrived, our ship was literally surrounded by small boats, filled to the brim with tropical fruits, which were offered at fabulously low prices. Many of us went into town and from sheer boredom had dinner at a Mexican hotel which we later regretted, for they charged us three dollars each for a supper consisting of roast chicken, salad, escargot, and fruits. I do not really blame the Mexican innkeeper for taking advantage of an opportunity that does not occur every day.

We left at three in the morning of April 22, after taking on an additional 214 passengers coming from Vera Cruz, Mexico City, and the interior of the country. Thus, our total number rose to 1,810, including 150 members of the ship's crew, all of whom arrived safely at our destination, with the exception of a merchant from Bremen who died the following day, April 23, and who was buried at sea with the customary ceremonies.

The body was sewn into a canvas bag, taking on the shape of an Egyptian mummy, and a twelve-pound cannon ball was tied to its feet. At two bells the entire ship's company assembled with heads bared; the captain made a short speech and from his prayer book conducted an Episcopalian funeral service. At three bells two sailors heaved the body into the depths from the top deck.

Before we left Acapulco, the local agent of the steamship company informed the captain that in Manzanillo, a ship's captain from Hamburg wished to have money transported and it was decided to go there and take on the consignment. On the night of April 23 we pulled safely into Manzanillo, a port in northern Mexico, but it was dark and we could not see the city.

Captain Feldman, who invited me among others to his ship, *Teodore*, where he treated us with true Hamburgian hospitality, informed me that Manzanillo has 15,000 inhabitants and that there are very rich silver mines nearby. Besides that, about four million cowhides are shipped annually from here.

Captain Feldman and his ship traveled 164 days from Hamburg, bringing firearms, silks, cotton goods, and all kinds of trinkets. He converted the entire shipment into cash and handed over to our captain $1,200,000 in gold, to be transported to the consignee in Hamburg. It will take weeks before he himself will leave for home, via Australia. He will take the silver bars to Australia and skins and hides to his home.

We continued our voyage on April 24 at three in the morning, and just as we fell into a deep sleep, two cannon shots woke us with a start. Frightened, we ran on to the deck in our nightshirts, only to find that our fear was baseless. There was no trouble; it was only two ships passing and greeting each other. Both ships stopped their engines, 175 and being no more than 100 paces apart, our captain went over to the *John Stevens* in a small boat and brought back many newspapers from San Francisco, as well as the information that its 874 passengers were all well.

The same day we reached the "Purple Sea"* at 21° 31′ N. latitude and 108° 16′ W. longitude, and crossing the Gulf of California at eight-thirty in the evening, we sighted from the distance Cape St. Lucas, the southernmost tip of California. By noon the next day we steamed by the Santa Margarita Islands, and on the twenty-sixth we saw the Santa Ambrosia Islands towards the northeast. These islands are all barren rocks, uninhabitable because of the lack of water.

On April 27 in the evening we left San Diego behind, and on the twenty-eighth we sighted San Pedro. By noon of April 29 we were near Monterey, steaming close to the shore, and from there on we sailed about two miles from the land. The coastline is low lying and marshy, with jagged, volcanic mountains in the background and without any vegetation. Beyond these, the mountains rise high in the distance, topped by the snowcapped peaks of the Sierra Nevadas.

Yesterday, the thirtieth, at six in the evening, the San Francisco pilot climbed on board, and at seven we were already at Point Lobos, which is the entrance to San Francisco Bay. As we steamed into the bay, a beautiful sight greeted us. The mirror-like waters of the spacious harbor were jam full of ships and boats of all descriptions, flying the flags of almost every nation in the world. The bay is protected by three forts and amply provided with lighthouses.

The sun was just setting when we tied up at our berth in the very center of the town and came ashore. I have been here too short a time to describe the city, so I will have to leave that to some future date. Right now I just want to note that the distance from New York to Jamaica is 1,485 miles, and to Aspinwall 2,019 miles; from Panama to Acapulco, 1,416; to Manzanillo, 1,790 and to San Francisco 3,340 miles.

The total distance I have traveled from New York to San Francisco adds up to 5,427 miles.

Considering that we traveled on two steamships and one train, stopped five times and yet completed the trip in twenty-four days, it is unquestionably a triumph of civilization.

---

*Euphemism for the Gulf of California.

As to the cost of transportation, it is in keeping with the magnitude of the undertaking. The fare from New York to San Francisco is $300, to which one should add twenty-five dollars for incidental expenses.

Now then, if anyone wants to make a calculation by multiplying the number of passengers by $300, adding $10,000 which every ship receives from the government for every voyage for transporting the mail, plus approximately $40,000 revenue from freight, one can form some idea of how profitable this is for the steamship company, even if half of the amount were earmarked for "expenses."

San Francisco,
May 5, 1857

Dear Mother:

Although there is nothing much new I can write at this time, I don't want to miss the opportunity to say a few words, as the mail is leaving this evening for the United States and Europe, on the ship *Golden Gate*.

San Francisco and its harbor are very well situated and the view from the ocean is indeed picturesque, but as the stranger roams over its streets he is soon disappointed. The location of the city is very similar to Pressburg* [Pozsony], except that the hills come close to the shore here. This circumstance makes it difficult to build on the rocky hillsides; consequently, one-third of the city is built on the sea. The houses rest on pillars and the sea is literally under 140 of its streets. At high tide the water rises almost to the flooring, and at ebb tide, if one should lift a joist or a floorboard and look below, one would see mud, rats, and frogs under the rooms, under the streets and everywhere.

Given these circumstances, one would think that the city would be unhealthy, but this is not the case at all. It is common knowledge that San Francisco is one of the healthiest cities in the world, which is probably due to the fact that daily, between one and seven in the afternoon, at high tide, a fresh, northwest breeze blows and cleans the air.

*Present day Bratislava.

One-third of the city is built in the aforementioned manner, and another third on the hillsides, just like the shacks on Gellért Hill or the Zuckermandl in Pressburg; and the rest is built on shifting sand dunes in the eastern part of the city.

While the expanse of the city is vast, most of it is not yet built up, although from the higher elevations one can clearly see the streets running at right angles. Some of the streets are so grand, with their stone and brick buildings and stores, that they can compete with any European city, but a large part of the city consists of wooden shacks, with the very natural result that there are two to three fires evey day, which, being so commonplace, are ignored by all except those in jeopardy.

The city's population of 84,000 is a mixture of every nationality in the world, yet it can be divided into four major groups—one-fourth English-speaking, one-fourth part French and Spanish, one-fourth German, and one-fourth Chinese. The rest are an insignificant combination of minorities.

These last (the Chinese) have a special status. When gold was discovered in California in 1848, San Francisco had a population of only 1,200, and the entire state of California, only 12,000. The mining companies needed a labor force. White labor was too expensive and slavery was prohibited. The attention of the capitalists was therefore directed to the great proletarian masses of China. Many ships were dispatched and in a few years about 40,000 Chinese were imported; at first they worked very cheaply, but later, when they became acquainted with the local conditions, they demanded higher and higher wages, and soon they expected to be paid as much as the whites.

Thus, the children of the Celestial Empire soon became affluent and independent. At present there are 22,000 in San Francisco alone, where they live in a separate section and are engaged in every kind of business imaginable. They have three Chinese newspapers, their own opera house, and a dance hall. Noteworthy is the fact that they have kept their original style of clothing to this day and show no disposition at all to adopt themselves to Western civilization.

When one walks in the Chinese quarter one can easily believe oneself to be in China. Chinese ideograms are written in the gaudiest colors on every house and store; the Chinese language and music can be heard everywhere; the sons and daughters of the Heavenly Kingdom shuffle about in their small, peaked caps, loose tunics, wide

178

trousers, and tiny thick-soled footwear, their long braids reaching almost to the ground.

That the Chinese quarter is full of saloons, bordellos, and all kinds of institutionalized prostitution does not speak well for the moral standards of the Heavenly Kingdom.

Museums, academies, libraries, or any other kind of cultural institution are nonexistent in San Francisco. Apparently there has been as yet no time for such things, for no one here has leisure for book learning. Everybody is busy rushing about to acquire wealth and treasures. It appears to the attentive observer that everyone wants to live for today, as if the last judgment were at hand. On the street everyone runs, carriages and wagons gallop at full speed, and people wolf down their food. The last bite is not chewed before they are on the run again, constantly glancing at their watches. All night long there is music, dancing, whoring, dice and card playing, yet at sunrise the entire community is up and about.

The cultural level of society is necessarily low, given such a life style. The common laborer, who only a few weeks ago was stoking furnaces or digging ditches, became rich in the gold mines and rides today in a carriage, has a household staff, and is honored as a person of eminence.

The servant or cook who a short while ago was cooking, scrubbing and washing, today—because she has a pretty face—is the wife of a rich merchant or banker. The newly arrived barber's helper is a famous doctor here, and a common blacksmith's apprentice is a veterinarian, and so it goes.

Under such circumstances it is obvious that personal courage is not very prevalent. Unpunished murders and robberies occur daily everywhere, as if they were ordinary events, and no one can tell when normality may return to this society.

Outside of the three Chinese newspapers mentioned before, the press is represented by three German, two Spanish, three French and seventeen English dailies. There are also many weekly and semiweekly periodicals and a few monthly magazines.

It would be a mistake, however, to conclude that the people get cultural sustenance from such a large number of publications. Their content, without exception, excludes "reading" matter. One half is advertisement, one quarter, the daily market prices, financial quotations, and so on, and the rest is news from the mines, usually describing murder and mayhem. News of Europe and of world politics in general are seldom printed and then only in a few short lines.

San Francisco's commerce is flourishing, and from its port not only every part of America but all parts of the world can be reached. There are weekly sailings to Australia, China, Marseilles, and Liverpool. Coastal steamers go to Oregon in the north and to the Americas in the south, and of course there is very close contact with the rest of California.

San Francisco Bay is actually formed by the estuary of the Sacramento River, which is navigable by steamer for nearly 300 miles upstream. On the shores of the river are Benicia, Sacramento City, Marysville, Nevada, and Stockton, all important and rapidly growing towns. There is a lively steamboat traffic between them and San Francisco, intensified by the heavy stagecoach traffic between these towns and the various gold mines.

I will write more fully about this after I have visited the placer-mining camps and fields.

Coastal steamers go weekly to the north as far as the estuary of the Columbia River and to the south to San Diego. I plan to travel on this same line to San Pedro and on muleback with our whole party through Los Angeles to Tejon in the Sierra Nevada mountains; but before that I will want to visit the gold mines, if possible.

The large amounts of money in circulation and the ease of acquiring it has reduced its value. The smallest coin in circulation is twelve-and-a-half cents, which is the cost of a sewing needle, a cigar or a glass of beer.

Clothing and footwear are comparatively inexpensive, but food is more costly than anywhere in the world. For example, a chicken costs over two dollars, a dozen eggs about eighty-five cents, a pound of beef one dollar, a pound of potatoes twenty-five cents, a pound of cabbage thirty-five cents, a pound of cauliflower eighty-five cents and so forth. To have one dozen articles of personal laundry (socks, shirts, handkerchiefs, and so on laundered) costs five dollars. Board and room in the inns costs three dollars a day, sixteen dollars a week and fifty dollars a month.

In closing my letter, I note with pleasure that all our compatriots who lived and are still living here acquired wealth. My friend Molitoris, who emigrated here from London back in 1851, returned last year with his sacks of gold. He was a money-changer here, and very sensibly he went to Europe to enjoy his wealth while he could.

At present there are four compatriots who still live here. John Szabo, who is a secretary at the federal mint, has a very high salary and considerable capital invested in various enterprises.

Our countryman, the famous adventurer, Augustin Haraszthy, together with Count Vas and Urnay, a former captain of the militia, own a bank and a money-changing establishment. They also own a steam-operated gold smelter and refinery, and although their business is just beginning to flourish, they are already millionaires.

Haraszthy's son [Árpád] came with me on the boat from New York. He is still only a child, and has come directly from the Bácska* to join his older brother to try his fortune. I have not met Urnay yet, but I met his wife yesterday in the bank. She is a Hungarian lady from Ujvidék and she cordially invited me for dinner, which I gladly accepted, especially because she invited other compatriots in my honor.

Urnay lives outside of the city at the Santos Dolores Mission. I understand that he has a large, castle-like home in a very nice English style park. He comes home in his carriage in the evening only, as he spends all day in the city.

I have had a very pleasant encounter here, which I want to tell you about. I met Madame Hueber, who had received me in Hamburg with so much sisterly affection. Henrietta was telling me that her husband emigrated here in 1852 and transferred his business here; however, he died last year. Henrietta, being a rich widow and young and attractive, naturally does not lack suitors. She is a cultured and witty lady and does not want to bury herself here; therefore, she is returning this summer to Hamburg. Last night I met the entire local civilized German community at her home, and after getting to know the German dandies, I am not surprised that she wants to flee from them all the way to Hamburg.

Los Angeles, Southern California
July 1, 1857

Dear Mother:

I hope by now that you have received my letter written from San Francisco on May 1. I should have liked to have written since then,

---

*The southern district of Hungary, now part of Yugoslavia.

but, so help me God, it was impossible. On May 5 I received from the department a six-weeks vacation for travel. I left immediately for Oregon and sailed all the way to the waterfalls of the majestic and wonderfully wild Columbia River where, in the company of beaver hunters, I crossed Mount Hood on muleback to Humboldt Bay. There I joined another hunting party, with which I traveled on horseback to the Sacramento River, from which they were heading to the Rocky Mountains. Since my route diverged from theirs, we parted company, and the same day I arrived in Marysville, which is the most northeasterly mining town in California.

From there I went to Sacramento City, the state capital, then to Stockton and finally to the eastern gold mines, where I have observed the entire process and carefully examined the method of placer mining and drawn many sketches and maps and filled a notebook with my scribbling. From Stockton via Red Bluff I have returned to San Francisco, where I arrived on the night of June 21.

Mother, you cannot imagine how tired I was after this excursion. For two whole days I did nothing but sit on a couch in my hotel balcony, smoking and eating ice cream. (It was very hot here.) Several times I picked up pen and paper to write to you, but it was impossible. My knees shook, my hands were numb, and the blast of shotguns, the roar of bears, and the bellow of panthers were constantly echoing in my ears.

The two days of *dolce far niente*, however, completely restored me and I feel as well as if I had only taken a stroll in the country.

On the twenty-fourth of last month, following my departmental orders, I boarded a steamer again and sailed down the coast of the Pacific Ocean. On the same day we arrived at Monterey, the former capital of California, where we spent the whole day.

On the twenty-fifth we dropped anchor at San Luis Obispo, where we loaded and unloaded.

On the twenty-sixth we reached Santa Barbara.

On June 27 I came ashore at San Pedro, while the boat continued on to San Diego. We had a great deal of trouble disembarking, for the harbor is a very poor one, and also a contrary wind was blowing so that the steamer could not get near the coast. A small fishing barge came for us, but we had not gone halfway when it ran aground and, having no alternative, we all jumped into the water and in waist-deep water and ankle-deep sand dragged the barge for half a mile until at last we reached deep water and were able to land.

13. *Eastern View of San Gabriel Mission, South California*, original drawing by Xántus, July 2, 1857; print by Rohn, Pest, 1858.

By that time it was late at night, and after our involuntary bath a cleanup was needed, so I had to stay in San Pedro, which is a kind of place like the country inn (*csárda*) where we once had to stay on our way from Tolna, fleeing the flood. Do you remember it, mother? However, instead of roast duck I had roasted rats for supper; instead of eiderdown I slept on a dirty reed mat; and for these comforts I paid three dollars in the morning.

On the morning of the twenty-eighth I hired three mules and, starting eastward in the afternoon, reached Los Angeles the same night, which was the meeting place of our entire company.

However, when I arrived on July 1 the company was scattered all over the vicinity hunting, and even though I put forth every effort, I was still unable to find them.

At last, yesterday noon I rode over to the San Gabriel Mission, where I found most of our expedition drinking wine and playing monte with the pious fathers in the refectory of the monastery. After handshakes all around, since I did not want to drink or play cards, I left, in the company of a young friar who showed me the cloister, the gardens, and all the mission buildings. The cloister and the church are built of massive carved stone blocks and are very attractive.

About 140 Indian families live in the various annexes, and all speak, read and write Spanish.

They are also artisans engaged in different crafts, such as blacksmith, carpenter, tailor, harness-maker, wood-carver, and shoemaker. They work in well equipped workshops, both for the mission and themselves.

The married ones have separate little houses, consisting of a living room, bed room, and kitchen, built of adobe and roofed with tile shingles.

The single ones live in a separate large house with two people sharing a bedroom and common dining room.

The girls weave, sew, wash, and live in a house completely apart, under the supervision of four nuns, who, between us, are pretty little women, very kind and who don't run from you, like the ones in Varasd, but show the guests around, walking arm in arm.

The garden, which is about 500 acres, is fenced by a ten-foot-high and six-foot-wide adobe wall, outside of which is a six by six (feet) deep trench surrounded by an awesome cactus hedge, in which even a porcupine would be stuck, should it attempt to cross.

The garden inspires admiration by all who appreciate beauty, comfort and utility. It is a rectangle which is bisected by two main roads. In the center of the garden there is a huge water basin 200 feet in diameter, built of carved stone. From a nearby river, water can be let in or out of the basin through well-maintained stone irrigation ditches, which crisscross the garden. This basin is used to stock and breed thousands of fine fish, and also to irrigate the garden.

Large orange trees are planted alongside the roads, which are heavy with fruit all year round and which form a beautiful, shady, tree-lined avenue, through which sunshine barely penetrates.

One entire section is planted exclusively with grapes, which grow in such abundance that the mission sells 500 barrels of wine annually, not taking into account its own consumption.

A second section is planted with greens, maize, barley, and potatoes. A third is planted with sugar cane and the fourth with banana, almond, pomegranate, and fig trees. The entire interior fencing consists of lemon trees, which are trimmed to the same height as the adobe wall.

The garden is under the supervision of a special group, the members of which work alternately, but only from four to eight in the morning and from four to eight in the evening.

The mission also owns 2,000 horses and mules and 5,000 cattle, which graze on its ten-square-mile property under the care of cowboys and shepherds on horseback. The pasture is equally good winter or summer and so the herd is in the mountains all the time, except for the service animals.

All this great wealth belongs to the mission, and every Indian (the "redeemed flock," as the saintly fathers call them) enjoys the fruits of communal labor and diligence. Part of the yearly surplus sold is spent on improvements, another part to buy clothing and colonial goods, and the remainder is put into the missions fund, which is under the jurisdiction of the Bishop of Monterey.

Returning to the refectory with my guide, Padre Bernardo, I found my friends huddled in a corner, still playing cards. (The table was already set for a meal.) Soon the bell rang, and to show our appreciation for the hospitality of our generous hosts, we partook of the princely repast with a hearty appetite. The mission wine is very good, but very strong—so strong that some of my friends were completely off their feet. We had to stay overnight at the mission, and only this morning did we arrive in the little town of Puebla.

Los Angeles, with a population of 500, lies on a beautiful plain on 185 both sides of a river of the same name and offers a very pleasing view. With the exception of the western side, where the bare plain is filled with salty lagoons, it spreads as far as the Pacific Ocean. It is surrounded on all sides by high mountains. In the background glitter the snowcapped peaks of the Sierra Nevada.

The little town also grows many grapes and tropical fruits and is engaged in an extensive trade in leather goods. It is also the seat of the judiciary of Southern California.

Our entire company of 185 people was divided into four groups. Fifty are leaving tomorrow to reconnoiter the Mesilla Valley and the Gadsden territory. (This area was purchased two years ago for $2,000,000 by the Union from the Mexican Republic.) Fifty will also leave tomorrow for San Diego, from there to survey the border between southern and lower California. A third party of seventy-four people is staying here, and will be split into small groups to start surveying the territory in order to form townships and sections from the seacoast inward, according to American custom.

Next week on the fourteenth we shall start for Fort Tejon, the headquarters of the corps, where a drafting and map-making bureau is going to be established. This will again be divided into three sections. I will be in charge of one of them, the croquis department, with five draftsmen under me.

Fort Tejon is 165 miles from here, and the road is beset with difficulties. We have to cross snow-covered mountains where it is impossible to travel with wagons. Our baggage and tools have to be packed in small sacks to be loaded on mules and burros. The government has arranged to have our mail delivered every fifteen days, so there will be no interruption in our correspondence.

I have just been informed by the postmaster that he has sent some fifty letters to Tejon for me last week, among which were many from Europe. So I hope, dear mother, that your last letters will be waiting for me; needless to say, I am looking forward to them very much.

I don't know if I shall have the time to describe my excursions from San Francisco, which were so rich in adventure. I should have liked to write about them now in more detail, but truly I don't know where to start. My head is so full of recent happenings that once I start, I couldn't stop and would write pages and pages, for which I really don't have the time at present. But I shall soon have more time at my disposal, I hope, and then I shall tell you all about my experiences and adventures.

Los Angeles, Southern California

July 5, 1857

Dear Mother!

Since we are not leaving until tomorrow evening, I shall use this time to write once more before reaching my destination. We had quite a bit of trouble with the preparation of tools and cases to be loaded onto the animals; that is why we spent so much time here.

The local flora is truly splendid. It is hard to imagine more beautiful and colorful plants and flowers than the ones here in the valleys and meadows.

I picked a tuft of wildflowers in San Gabriel and pressed them in a book, so that I could send one in each of my letters to give you an idea of how beautiful and varied is the local plant life.

Let us leave the local scene for the moment and let me take you, dear mother, on wings of thought, once again to San Francisco. I do not know when I shall have time to write again of my experiences there, and there are enough to fill volumes.

I will acquaint you with an enterprise of our compatriots, of which every Hungarian could be justifiably proud. It is the gold smeltery of Counts Vas, Urnay and Haraszthy. My friend Vas took me to the factory and was kind enough to show and explain every nook and corner of it. I was amazed at the compact equipment and its extensive, economical, and practical operation.

The factory buildings are about two miles from his house, on the main square at the corner of Harris and Brennan Streets and occupy an eight-acre area. There are two main branches—gold refining and metallurgy. The first is in a compact stone building, which is so elegant, in the true sense of the word, that any Hungarian magnate could use it for his palace. It is 400 feet long, 152 feet wide and sixty-two feet high, and built on a hill, and the entire space between the walls and the street is partitioned into formal flower beds, which give the entire building a delightful appearance.

The building is again divided into several sections, the chief ones 187 of which are refining, smelting, and granulating rooms; then come the classifying and testing chambers, and then again the different offices and vaults to safeguard the treasures.

As one enters the building through the main gate, one steps into a room where the gold dust and granules are weighed.

The east and west sides of this room are made of glass, through which the chief inspector can oversee the workers in every part of the building. Everything is weighed here on four large bank scales, and a long table is covered with small metal boxes, into which the different grades of gold are temporarily deposited until they are taken into custody either here or in the city office.

From this same room the refined gold bars, appropriately stamped, are consigned to be used as the medium of exchange, for jewelry, and so on.

Adjoining this room is the main vault, which is burglar proof and fireproof and in which there is a huge, indestructable metal box.

Behind this room is the office of Vas, which is a small sanctum furnished with excellent taste. I say sanctum advisedly, for the walls are lined with gold-framed pictures of great Hungarian writers and publicists, who I am sure collectively have never seen as much treasure at home as they see sharing the room with Vas.

Before I tell you about the operation of this institution, I would like to mention its accomplishment so far. One hundred-and-twenty-two workers and a sixty-horsepower engine are in motion day and night—the process never stops—with the result that in a single day 27,000 ounces of gold are refined. The average daily net result is 18,000 troy ounces of refined gold. Ninety-four thousand ounces were refined during the week of my visit. The refined gold is then poured into bars alloyed with copper for the mint, and into pure, fishbone-thin rods for the trade and for shipment to Europe.

The refining room occupies the western part of the building and is eighty-two feet by fifty-two and the height is the same as that of the building. In this section is the steam engine, and numerous kettles, cauldrons, and ovens. One would think that the intense fire and the great variety of chemicals would make the room extremely hot, but the astonished visitor finds that just the opposite is true; for the entire room is ventilated by twelve to twenty-five foot-high windows, through which the city's westerly winds circulate freely.

On the western side, seven huge granulating cauldrons are set up with a capacity of 250 pounds of ore, which are boiled in sulfuric acid

14. *Los Angeles, California, Main Street and Church;* original drawing by Xántus, July 2, 1857; print by Rohn, Pest, 1857

for six hours prior to refining. From here the silver content is extracted into large troughs, where it is heated by steam for a certain length of time and, when liquified, piped into large tubs covered with copper plates, one end of which hangs into the content of the tub.

This procedure forces the silver into an ore-like form again, in this condition resembling sulfur and lead mixed clay. This ore mixture is then put into a hydraulic press in forms resembling a loaf of cheese. (The pressure is 19,000 pounds per square inch.) The loaves, pressed into paper thin form, are then broken into four pieces and put into drying ovens until completely dry.

By such operations the silver is completely recovered, which is a very important gain, because silver is an indispensable agent in gold refining. This, however, is not the only gain, for the copper portion is pumped into another tub, where, mixed with iron parts, it is precipitated into small, pure copper sheets.

During this procedure the gold is drawn into a pipe which is completely free from acid fumes. The room is lined with resinous material. The copper used here came from old ship bottoms, and, treated by the method described above, it is then marketed in far more refined and useful quality than when it was bought.

On the eastern side, one steps into the smelting and granulating room, which has a marble floor and eight large furnaces. Here the gold is granulated with silver before undergoing the operation described above. The ore leaves this room in tiny, popcorn-shaped globules, a shape acquired by precipitation in cold water.

South of this is the grading room, where there are three additional furnaces, one with an acid bath and one with a newly invented machine which produces essence needed to heat the ore to be graded.

On the west side of this room is yet another very small room (twelve square feet), which is the grader's weighing room, equipped with three scales, which are the wonders of human inventiveness in their sensitivity and accuracy. In my presence, Vas, with a pair of scissors, snipped off a microscopic segment of a bank note and placed it on one side of the scale, which immediately descended under the minuscule weight. Then he put gold dust on the other platter until they balanced. The gold dust weighed 1/4386 of a grain.

This room is full of slivers of gold in all shapes, all 1,000 proof without exception, that is, free of all impurities, for they are used as standards for grading.

On top of the building there is an endless number of tubs, supplied with water from an artesian well in the courtyard, for the needs of the factory.

The metallurgical buildings are on the north side of the area, with their numerous smelting furnaces, tall smokestacks and quartz-grinding mills. The quartz shipped here is first ground to powder in the mill, then in the furnace the ore is melted out of it under extremely high fire lasting four times twenty-four hours, after which it is further dispersed in another furnace. Only then is it processed in the other section, as described before.

It was during my visit that my friend Vas started the construction of a sixth impressive building in which only copper will be smelted and refined. There is a crying need for such operations in California, for until now copper was sent to Europe to be refined; but also it will be a very profitable undertaking, or so I hope with all my heart.

Although I tried (all too briefly) to make the tremendous undertaking of our countrymen intelligible to you, I am afraid my description is not as precise as I should like it to be, for statistics aside, I had to write it all from memory. I want to mention, moreover, that this refinery started operations only last February 13. Since that time it has refined $450,000,000 worth of gold and graded $250,000,000 worth.

During the time I was visiting there they were extremely busy, as the government mint was not in operation due to the presidential election. My friend Vas assured me that he had not gone to bed for nine nights, for his personal supervision was needed day and night.

The processes of this factory are not new inventions, although at present it is the only one in the world in operation; there is a similar one in Paris, but it refines only silver. In London, a Mr. Jones started one working at the time gold was discovered in Australia, but after wasting much time and money, he gave it up.

A Hungarian magnate* (Vas called him a "Judge of the King's bench), after experimenting for eight years, was finally able to cut the Gordian knot, so that now he can convert the treasure of California into a commercial medium of exchange so cheaply that no private or government establishment can compete with him.

Such an enterprise deserves to be successful and richly rewards the investment of sleepless nights and several hundred thousand

*Count Ágoston Haraszthy.

dollars. This enterprise is the most remarkable one on the Pacific Coast and we Hungarians can be justly proud of Count Vas and his partners, who represent our homeland with so much distinction in one of the greatest nations of the world.

In San Francisco there is also a Hungarian barber named Csapkay, a fabulous humbug the like of which has not appeared yet among our emigrés. Ever since he came to San Francisco penniless, he has circulated grandiose brochures and advertisements in every newspaper, claiming he was a great physician in Hungary and that he is able to cure every imaginable disease instantly. The number of his patients has increased from day to day, so that by now he has attained the position of something of an oracle.

During my stay in San Francisco this charlatan was flourishing, and as he stated, he has already amassed several hundred thousand dollars by his quackery. He also has a very nice house in the best section of the city. It is remarkable how easily you can fool the American public, if you find the "right way." I have never met a clumsier and more ignorant lad than this Csapkay, yet he has succeeded. From one of the German papers I clipped his advertisement, which is not quite as bold and absurd as the ones that appear in the American papers; for among the Germans one generally finds people of discernment, but the clipping will give you a chance to judge him for yourselves, without any further comment from me. I know you will get a good laugh, particularly when he claims to be able to help *Kinderlosigkeit* (infertility).

Enough of this impostor who would bring only disgrace to the good name of our beloved Fatherland. I shall keep you informed of my further travels and discoveries. In the meantime keep well and God bless you.

After the publication of his Letters *in Hungary, Xántus continued writing. His second book,* Travels in the Southern Parts of California, *was published in Pest in 1860. It is a colorful narrative of his assignment at Fort Tejon and his exploration of Baja California. The book is divided into three parts: the first describes the journey from Los Angeles to Fort Tejon; the second, entitled "Tejon and the Tejon* *Indians," is a detailed description of conditions at Fort Tejon and its vicinity; and the third, "The California Peninsula," is an account of an expedition by sea from San Diego to San Bartolome Bay on the west coast of Baja California. Proceeding from there overland to La Paz along a route near the west coast, Xántus went from La Paz back to San Bartolome Bay overland along the gulf coast, then by sea to San Diego. Lively sketches abound: Loreto, Todos Santos, La Paz, the flora and fauna, the people. A short essay on early Spanish explorations and Aztec antiquities by János Hunfalvy, a noted Hungarian ethnologist and Xántus's literary agent, forms the concluding chapter. And the final pages contain an appeal by Xántus on behalf of the Smithsonian Institution, expressing its desire to exchange scientific specimens collected by Americans with those collected by their Hungarian counterparts. The American specialists mentioned include: Spencer Baird, John L. LeConte, Joseph Leidy, Edward Hallowell, Thomas Brewer, William A. Hammond, and John Cassin—all naturalists associated with Xántus as collectors.*

To quote from Xántus's foreword to Travels in the Southern Parts of California:

I must note that the present book represents only a fraction of my journey in California. The pace of life is so rapid in America that communication lags behind events. I have not yet organized the part of my voyage dealing with northern California and Oregon. I had scarcely begun to do that when I became involved in southern California with an entirely different group of people and their life style.

Now, once again, I start on a new trek, and by the time these lines are in print, I shall be wandering in the Cordilleras of western Mexico. I hasten to publish these segments while I may, and hope that they will be well received if for no other reason than because as yet the land and the peoples described here are completely unknown in Hungarian literature. I am fully conscious of the many shortcomings of this work, especially from the standpoint of style. Still, it may provide the reading public with some knowledge and pleasure. And at least it accounts for the way I have spent precious time so far away from my beloved country.

Canon del Tejon, California   John Xántus
October 5, 1858

Bibliography

Cholnoky, Eugene. "In Memory of John Xántus." *Bulletin of the Hungarian Geographic Society*. Budapest, 1925. Pp. 210–12.

Dictionary of American Biography, s.v. "Xántus, János."

Essig, Edward Oliver. *A History of Entomology*. New York: Macmillan, 1931.

György, Aladar. "Xántus János." *Bulletin of the Hungarian Geographic Society*. Budapest, 1894. Pp. 337–81.

Harris, Harry. "Notes on the Xántus Tradition." *Condor* 36 (1934): 191–201.

Hume, Edgar Erskine. *Ornithologists of the United States Army Medical Corps: Thirty-six Biographies*. Baltimore: Johns Hopkins Press, 1942.

Lantos, Louis. "John Xántus: A Memorial." *Natural Science Bulletin* 67 (1935): 467–71.

Lengyel, Emil. *Americans from Hungary*. Philadelphia: Greenwood Press, 1948.

Madden, Henry Miller. *Xántus, Hungarian Naturalist in the Pioneer West*. Palo Alto, Cal.: Books of the West, 1949.

Mocsáry, Sándor. "In Memory of John Xántus: Eulogies." *Proceedings, Hungarian Academy of Science*. Budapest, 1899, Pp. 231–58.

Palmer, Theodore Sherman. "Notes on Persons Whose Names Appear in the Nomenclature of California Birds." *Condor* 30(1928): 261–307.

Pivány, Eugene. *Hungarian-American Historical Connections*. Budapest, 1927.

Rodgers, Andrew Denny. *John Torrey: A Story of North American Botany*. Princeton, N.J.: Hafner, 1942.

Smithsonian Institution. *Annual Reports for the Years 1856–1864.*

Steinbeck, John, and Ricketts, Edward F. *Sea of Cortez*. New York: Viking Press, 1941.

Szinnyei, Joseph. *Lives and Works of Hungarian Writers*. Vol. 14. Budapest, 1914.

Index

196

John Xántus (1825–1894), a political refugee after the unsuccessful Hungarian revolution of 1848, came to America in 1851. He rose from obscurity to fame as a naturalist and collector of the western frontier. His letters to his family report in detail the incidents of his daily life, the organization of his expeditions, and his journeys through the unexplored wilderness.

Theodore Schoenman and Helen Benedek Schoenman, the translators, share an interest in political refugees from Hungary who came to America in the years preceding the Civil War. Their translation of Xántus's Travels in Southern California *is forthcoming from the Wayne State University Press.*

The book was designed by Julie Paul. The typeface for the text is Caledonia designed by W. A. Dwiggins about 1938; and the display face is Caslon Old Style with swash caps based on the original design by William Caslon in the eighteenth century.

The text is printed on EB Booknatural paper, and the book is bound in Columbia Mills Fictionette cloth over binders boards.

Manufactured in the United States of America.